# Wartime Cheshire
## 1939 - 1945

# CHESHIRE

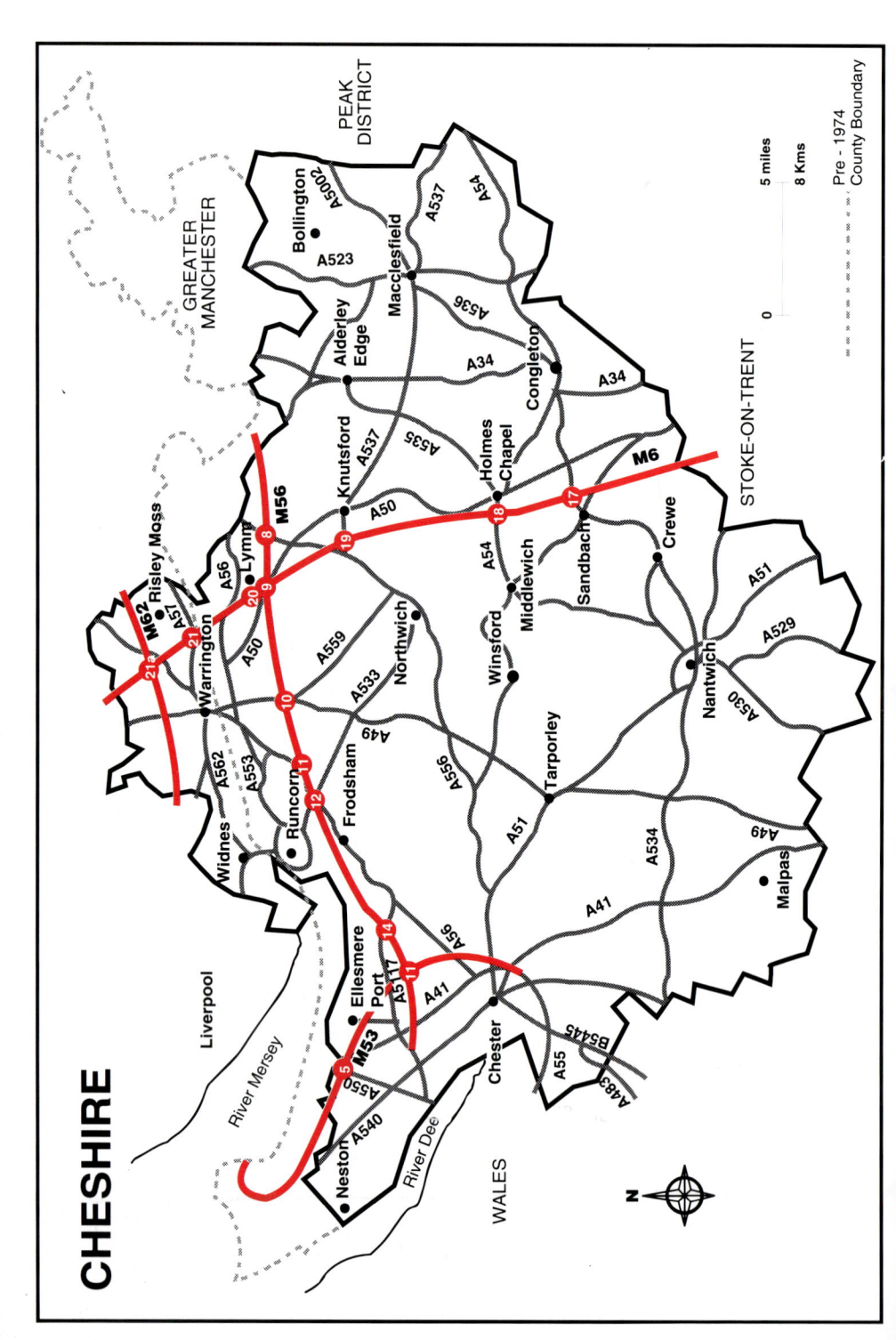

# Wartime Cheshire 1939 - 1945

## Contents

| | |
|---|---|
| Cheshire's Role in the War | 4 |
| Chester at War - Castle, Cathedral and Cinemas | 9 |
| An ABC of the Chester and Ellesmere Port Areas - Animals, Boats and Camps | 17 |
| The Nantwich District - Agriculture and Evacuees | 25 |
| Vale Royal - Tanks, Troops and a Night of Terror | 33 |
| Northwich-Runcorn-Widnes - Chemicals in Wartime | 39 |
| Crewe at War - Smoke Screen and Balloon Barrage | 47 |
| *A Memorial to Courage* | Centre pages i to viii |
| Warrington - Arms, Airmen and Americans | 55 |
| The Knutsford Area in Wartime - Men Dropping from the Skies | 63 |
| Ringway and the Airborne Forces - The Great Innovation of World War II | 73 |
| Macclesfield at War - Silk Mills and Stone Quarries | 85 |
| Capesthorne, Congleton and Sandbach - Convalescents, Dutchmen and Vehicles of War | 93 |
| Glossary | 100 |
| Index | 101 |

# Cheshire's Role in the War

When you think of the Second World War, do your thoughts mainly fly to the front line of battle, to the campaigns in North Africa, Middle East or Europe? Do you visualise the Battle of Britain fought in the skies of South-East England or the gallant convoys braving enemy U-Boats on the seas to help feed a nation? In your mind's eye do you see the blitz-weary cities of Liverpool, London, Coventry, Manchester, Glasgow and Plymouth amid fire and rubble?

All this would seem to have little to do with Cheshire, that essentially rural county in the North West of England, famed for its cheese and the grinning cat in Alice in Wonderland. But this guide is about the county in wartime and pays tribute to the men, women and children engaged on a very different battlefield - fighting day by day in the fields, factories, training camps, hospitals and homes to help defeat Hitler's Germany.

Ironically, Cheshire's lack of strategic importance in the eyes of German High Command was to make it a very important area to the British war effort. Safe from enemy bombing the county was to become a refuge for many evacuees from our cities and a training ground for the many servicemen and women of the British and Allied forces based in its camps and housed in its towns and villages.

The people of Cheshire were to cope with amazing efficiency and good will with both invasions. Thanks to the WVS, the local billeting officer and many volunteers, homes were found for thousands of frightened children and young mothers who suddenly found themselves in unfamiliar surroundings after a crowded and depressing train journey. The forces too, were welcomed and received much kindness and hospitality from the local people wherever they went.

The differences in background and lifestyle between the country folk and city dwellers were sometimes difficult to cope with. Some of the evacuees' health and hygiene gave cause for anxiety - as did sometimes their behaviour and morals. Some brought lice into clean homes, suffered from skin diseases and rickets while others thought it strange to go to bed before 11pm as they had been used to spending evenings on the street outside pubs waiting for their parents until closing time. Many had existed on a staple diet of chips and white bread and did not care for 'good home cooking'. One boy apparently thought it 'normal' to sleep under the bed and not in it - at home he didn't even have one of his own.

Teachers were often evacuated with their pupils and this helped relieve the pressures on households where evacuees were billeted. For the teachers though, it meant increased duties and extended hours and little or no holidays. Some schools and local organisations helped too with lunches every day to help ease the financial strain on local households. The allowances they received were not really enough when you consider that growing children need such things as new clothes and shoes - which parents were either unwilling or unable to provide. Again the WVS and voluntary bodies came to the

*Evacuees at Tilstone Fearnall, near Tarporley.*

rescue with second hand clothing. But in spite of these problems, the majority of children settled down well in the county enjoying the countryside and the fresh air and becoming healthier day by day.

Cheshire was also the **centre of military activity** during the war. Western Command was based at Chester and the Bickerton and Peckforton Hills became training grounds for the troops. All over the county military camps sprang up for training and to house the exiled forces of our European Allies, waiting to return and liberate their countries from Nazi domination. Soon Cheshire was 'home' for Dutch, Czech, Polish and French soldiers and airmen. In the months before the Normandy Landings, thousands of Americans swelled their ranks. Although there was some initial jealousy and distrust of these foreigners, they were generally welcomed into the community. The friendliness and generosity of the 'Yanks' are still remembered with affection today, and many still return to revisit their favourite pubs.

The county was to play a **key role in the defence of the North West**, with Anti Aircraft batteries dotted along the Mersey, and Manchester Ship Canal. Several RAF stations - Sealand, Hooton Park and Poulton, near Chester - were established together with the main North West Night Fighter defence base at Cranage. But perhaps the most exciting role that the county was to play was in the development of RAF Ringway, now Manchester International Airport. Here No. 1 Parachute Training School was established which was to play a major part in the preparation for the invasion of Europe by **training thousands of troops in the new skill** of parachute jumping - a key factor in modern warfare and essential to victory. *(See centre pages for a photographic souvenir of Cheshire's role in the training of Airborne Forces and special agents).*

The county was a **major food producer too**, a role which took on more importance as the war went on. Food imports became erratic and very costly thanks to the U-Boat activity in the Atlantic and the Axis/enemy occupation of many countries which normally supplied Britain with food and raw materials. Ordinary people were 'digging for victory' in their gardens while farmers struggled to produce livestock and more and more from the land in an attempt to make the country as self-sufficient as possible.

So, safety zone, military training ground, defence post and food-producer - and still Cheshire had more to offer the war effort. Though not primarily an industrial region, the county was one of the **major chemical producing areas** of Britain thanks to its natural resources of salt and brine, essential ingredients for many chemical processes. A thriving industry had been built up in the county since the 19th century using the canal and river network to bring salt to Runcorn and Widnes to feed the chemical factories situated there. Northwich had been the home of ICI since John Brunner and Ludwig Mond had set up their plant at Winnington. Some astute forward planning ensured that the industry was geared to meet the country's needs when war came, producing essential metal-cleaning solvents, explosive materials and polythene - perhaps the greatest contribution made by ICI to the war effort. Further east, on the Mersey at Risley Moss a huge munitions works sprang up, producing massive quantities of ammunition.

*Parachute training near Ringway. (Imperial War Museum).*

Cheshire did not altogether escape enemy bombs. It was not subjected to nightly bombardment like its near neighbours, Liverpool and Manchester, but it lay on the route of enemy bombers making for those cities. In the autumn and winter of 1940 particularly, German bombers often shed their load of bombs at random over the county if they failed to reach their main target. One such incident, on 28/29 November in that year, severely damaged the Tuberculosis Sanatorium at Barrowmore Hospital near Chester with 19 people killed and 30 injured. There were severe casualties at Crewe and Warrington too. Towards the end of the war, on Christmas Eve 1944, the only flying bombs aimed at the North West scored five hits in Cheshire but luckily only one caused casualties. Although we know the Luftwaffe had aerial photographs of the key installations such as gas and electricity works in the county, Cheshire was fortunately not high on the target list drawn up by German High Command.

To the south, around Crewe, was the **Rolls Royce 'Shadow' Factory**. 'Shadow' factories were built to duplicate vital production facilities so that supplies of components were unlikely to be totally cut off if one factory in the production chain was put out of action by bombs). This factory was set up to make aircraft engines - the famous 'Merlins'.

There were also **numerous small engineering workshops**. Crewe was a vital link in the railway system and its railway works was one of the country's key industrial producers. Further east at Sandbach, Fodens trucks went into increased production whilst in Macclesfield and Congleton, mills turned to producing textiles **(parachute silk and uniform cloths)** needed by the Forces.

These were not the only ways in which Cheshire and its people contributed to the national effort. Both men and women went off to join the Forces, leaving others behind to fill their places. They put every last ounce of energy into 'doing their bit' and at the same time tried to live their lives as 'normally' as possible. Many housewives went out to work for the first time, or joined voluntary Forces like the **Red Cross and WVS**. The **WIs** even gathered rosehips to help a national campaign to make syrup to supply vitamin C - in short supply as oranges and other fruit were a thing of the past! Remember that many children born in wartime had never seen an orange or banana!

*WI members joined in the war effort.*

Women joined knitting circles to provide troops with 'comforts' while men joined the **Home Guard,** training conscientiously and putting in many tedious hours of duty. Everyone had to live with the blackout, gas masks and rationing, plus the endless need to economise at home and to contribute to Government Savings Schemes like 'Wings for Victory' Week, 'Salute the Soldier' and 'Warship' and 'Spitfire Funds' to help finance the military effort.

Today, the steady march of progress since the early 1940s means that some places in this guide have changed beyond recognition, or have vanished entirely, but there is still much that has stayed the same.

*Czech encampment in Cholmondeley Park.*

Remember as you drive along the roads that in those days private cars were not as common as today, and the number in use in wartime was reduced by petrol rationing. Apart from buses, most of the traffic on these roads would have been military or commercial. So, if you can, imagine the roads generally peaceful - rather than today's rush and bustle. Try too, to imagine these towns and villages at night - all in total darkness, the cars struggling along with shaded lights and pedestrians cautiously feeling their way.

With this guide, it is easy to choose an area of the county, read of its main wartime events and visit the places that interest you. Though some sites may now be on private property, most are easily accessible. There really is a wealth of things to see and places to go - from stately home to industrial town, from country park to disused airfield. And it makes a novel way of exploring some of the significant features of our lovely county.

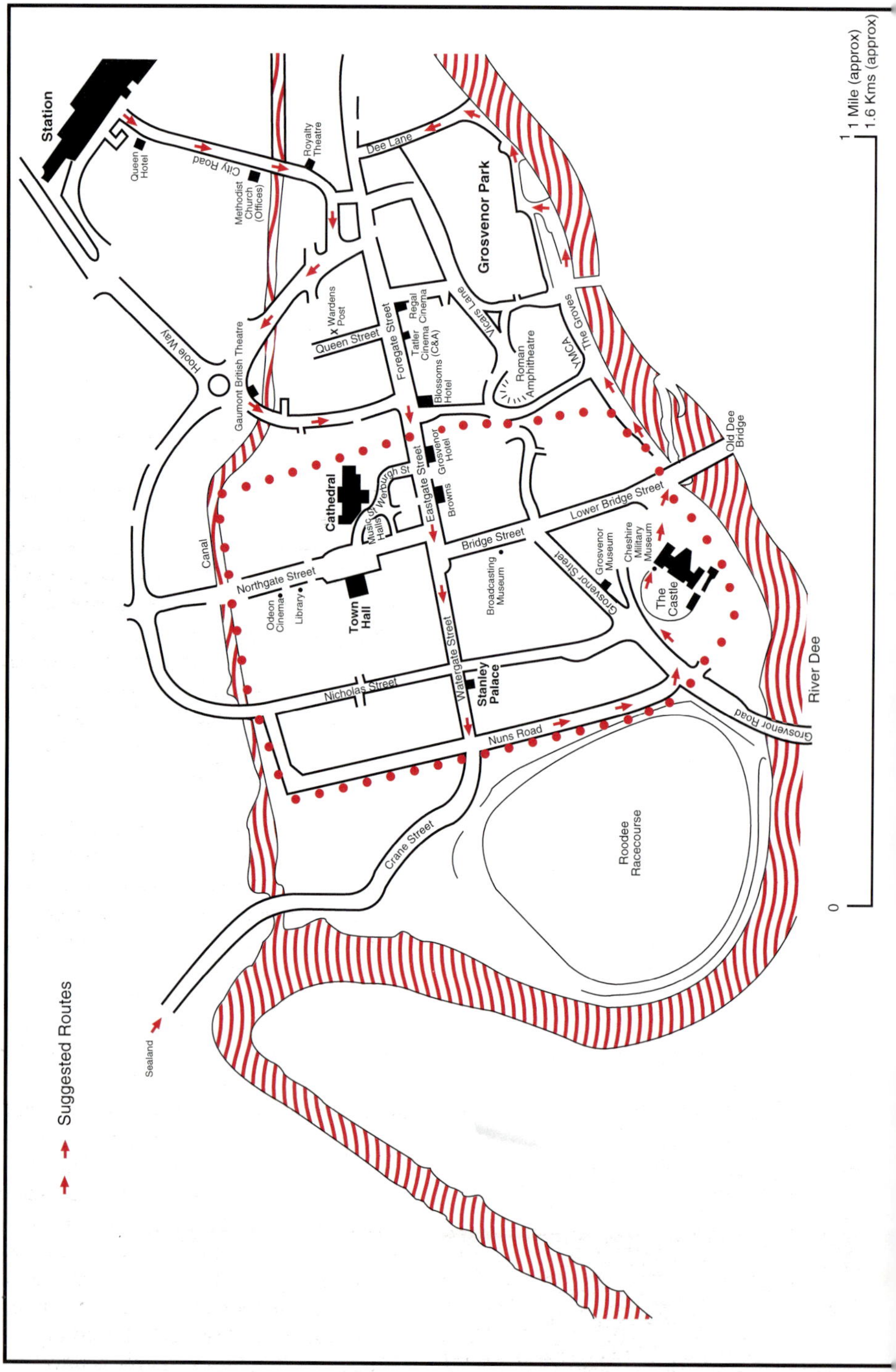

Station
Queen Hotel
City Road
Methodist Church (Offices)
Royalty Theatre
Dee Lane
Grosvenor Park
Hoole Way
Gaumont British Theatre
x Wardens Post
Queen Street
Foregate Street
Regal Cinema
Tatler Cinema
Blossoms (C&A) Hotel
Vicars Lane
Roman Amphitheatre
YMCA
The Groves
Old Dee Bridge
Grosvenor Hotel
Browns
Eastgate Street
Werburgh St
Cathedral
Music Halls
Canal
Northgate Street
Bridge Street
Lower Bridge Street
Grosvenor Museum
Cheshire Military Museum
Broadcasting Museum
Grosvenor Street
The Castle
Odeon Cinema
Library
Town Hall
Watergate Street
Stanley Palace
Nicholas Street
Nuns Road
Grosvenor Road
River Dee
Crane Street
Roodee Racecourse
Sealand
Suggested Routes
0
1 Mile (approx)
1.6 Kms (approx)

# Chester at War

## Castle, Cathedral and Cinemas

It was in 1938, when plans were formulated for the protection of civilians in the event of war, that Chester's own preparations began. All over the country, cities, towns and villages alike were anticipating the worst. By early 1939, air raid shelter designs were being approved, trenches dug and the first shelters erected. (Many of the country's air raid shelters were to come from the steelworks at nearby Shotton in North Wales.) So everywhere during the spring and summer of 1939, air raid precaution exercises and anti-gas drills were taking place.

*Public air raid shelter at the Church of Christ the King, Chester. (Chester Chronicle).*

War was declared in September 1939. Immediately reserve forces were called up, theatres and cinemas closed and blackout regulations enforced. Within 24 hours evacuees pouring out of Liverpool arrived at Chester station. The carefully planned war preparations had become reality. The well organised operation ran smoothly, but not without a certain amount of anxiety as people settled down to this new way of life. Soon though, the life of the city returned to normal - as far as wartime restrictions would allow.

'Business as usual' could have been Chester's wartime motto. Already a well-established shopping, entertainment and tourist centre, the city was determined to go on in its usual fashion. Although there were air raid alerts, after a few weeks passed, the shoppers, tourists and pleasure-seekers thronged the streets as before. There were public shelters against air attack available in the city centre - in the basements of The Blossoms Hotel and St. Michael's Arcade in the Rows, the vaults of the Oddfellows Hall in Bridge Street and the crypt of St. John's Church in Vicars Lane to name but a few. By late September that year, Wardens' posts were a familiar sight in the city too. Most of these are unrecognisable today because of re-development. The post situated in Watergate Street for example is now

(1995) B Wise store (opposite the black and white house with the words "God's Providence is mine inheritance" on its facade) but another, a private house at No. 16 Queen Street (opposite C&A in Foregate Street) looks much as it did during wartime.

Though local regiments spent most of the war overseas, Chester was still full of uniformed men and women. They mostly came from nearby camps, looking for a few hours' relaxation and entertainment whilst on leave. To meet their needs, theatres and cinemas were reopened and even some Sunday entertainment was permitted.

If you had been one such serviceman or woman on leave for the first time in the city, what would your impressions of Chester have been? Stepping off your train at this major railway junction, you might have had to push your way to the ticket barrier past crowds of service personnel waiting for trains to carry them to nearby training camps or further afield to ports for overseas embarkation. It would have been a relief to get through the barrier and out into the station concourse. So, you may have paused here for a while under the lovely Victorian facade with its ornamental stonework and then asked for directions to the town centre.

Pointed in the direction of City Road, you would start your walk down this main thoroughfare passing the QUEEN HOTEL on your left. Perhaps you might have stopped half way down the road to listen to the strains of a concert being held in the basement of the METHODIST CHAPEL on the right just before you crossed the canal. (Regular concerts for service personnel were held in this chapel during the war. Sadly the building is no more - it was demolished and replaced by offices). Past the canal now, on the opposite side of the road you may have paused to read the playbill of the Royalty Theatre, a popular place in wartime. Why, the Western Command's own amateur operatic group are performing 'Il Pagliacci' tonight! Not to your taste? Well, carry on to the end of City Road and turn right into the Cattlemarket (now part of the Ring Road) in search of other entertainments. Soon you will see the Gaumont-British Theatre (now Top Rank Bingo) just before you cross

*'Il Pagliacci' by Western Command. (Imperial War Museum).*

*Children met Tommy Handley, 1944. (Chester Chronicle).*

the canal at the top of Frodsham Street. As well as offering a varied programme for adult film-goers, you notice that it also runs a Saturday Club for children with celebrities like Tommy Handley paying regular visits.

Maybe this week's film does not appeal to you so walk down Frodsham Street and see what else Chester has to offer. If you turn left along Foregate Street you will find a Newsreel Theatre, called The Tatler, on the right (the site now occupied by C&A) and further along on the corner of Love Street, The Regal. Here in the heart of Chester's shopping centre, you are bound to dawdle in front of many shop windows like MARKS & SPENCER (still on the same site though much changed by modernisation) or the famous BROWNS OF CHESTER, a well-known independent store with a reputation for high quality goods. (Browns continued to advertise fur events, furniture events and seasonal fashions until late in 1942 when it ceased large scale advertising for the duration to help save newsprint.) Customers were received by an imposing uniformed commissionaire, and could be sure of the assiduous attention of immaculately turned out staff, even when rationing and 'coupons' made shopping difficult.

Though modernisation and redevelopment may have taken their toll of many of the old established shops these days, some do remain. Time for some refreshment now. Why not try the CHESTER GROSVENOR HOTEL in Eastgate - often the venue for formal regimental dinners and popular with wartime honeymooners, their time together made more precious by the war? Or how about the BLOSSOMS HOTEL on the corner of John Street where you can sit in a comfortable lounge and rest awhile? Many popular stage personalities stay here while visiting Chester - Bebe Daniels and Ben Lyon, Carroll Gibbons and his

*Wartime advertisement. (Chester Chronicle).*

band, Vic Oliver (Churchill's son-in-law), and Rene Houston to name but a few.

Considerably refreshed by now, the CATHEDRAL is your next port of call. Chester's Cathedral is famous and in these troubled times it is the spiritual heart of the city. It is here that people go to say a prayer for fallen comrades or loved ones far away. And it is here that servicemen stationed in the area and the men of the local civil defence often march for special church services on a National Day of Prayer. Are you surprised to see the wrought iron railings still intact? They have not fallen victim to the salvage drives to reclaim unused metal - unlike those at Grosvenor Park which did not have the same artistic merit! You might even be in time for one of the many concerts here by the Western Command's own symphony orchestra who often play host to visiting artists such as Pablo Casals, Dr Malcolm Sargent (later to become 'Sir') and the Hallé Orchestra, and Sir John Barbirolli. Today the Cathedral contains memorials to the RAF, and the Czech servicemen who

Cheshire County Salvage Drive. (Chester Chronicle).

were in Cheshire at this time.  Look underneath the stained glass window depicting St Werburgh which lies to the left of the visitors' entrance.  You can also visit the chapel dedicated to the Cheshire Regiment and outside, the Regiment's Garden of Remembrance.  Today the Cathedral is open every day except during services and you can visit its shop and Refectory restaurant.

   Leaving the Cathedral now you emerge into the sunlight and straight ahead you notice the Music Halls, a cinema in St Werburgh Street (these days The Reject Shop).  If you turn right now into Northgate Street you can see the fine Victorian TOWN HALL which houses the city's administrative and civic offices.  Here they organise Chester's welfare and safety.  You have heard that before the war a public address system was installed in the city which enabled concerts to be broadcast from the Town Hall and relayed along Eastgate Street and the Groves along the River Dee for people's enjoyment while out for a stroll.  (This happened particularly during savings campaigns such as 'Salute the Soldier' weeks when the people of Chester contributed huge sums to the national defence funds in addition to the regular penny a week schemes which most people belonged to.)

   To the right of the Town Hall you find yet another cinema.  This is the ODEON (still there today) where film-goers in Chester have a wide choice of films to see.  'Mrs Miniver' is playing at present and 'coming soon' are 'Gone with the Wind' and 'First of the Few' - which are bound to be retained for long runs.  Of course they have newsreels here too - you can never really escape the war, not even in the cinema!  Look - people are starting to go in for the afternoon performance - all carrying their gas masks in case there's an alert.  You've heard one story of the occasion when an alert sounded and the Management of the cinema decided to continue the show on the assumption that the 'All Clear' would sound fairly soon.  At the end of the film, however, the 'All Clear' had not been heard so it was impossible for patrons to leave.  The staff then played records to keep the audience entertained and when these ran out, they showed two horror films which the Government has issued to all cinemas to be shown in case of invasion (when regular film supplies would be disrupted).  Still the 'All Clear' did not sound.  In sheer desperation the projectionist put on the children's Mickey Mouse Club shows including Flash Gordon, episode 8.  Everyone concerned was utterly exhausted at the end of all this but as people left - the emergency over - many asked if they could have Flash Gordon again the next week!  Looking at the posters outside the Odeon now you can see that they and the

*Stanley Palace.*

*Members relax at the War Services Women's Club. (H. S. Woodward).*

'Gaumont British' also hold stage shows here for fund raising events during 'Salute the Soldier' or 'Warship' Weeks - some of these are even organised by Donald Piers whom you have heard is stationed at nearby Saighton Camp.

Why not continue your walk now back down Northgate Street and turn right along Watergate Street which also has some excellent shops. Further down, after you cross Nicholas Street, look out for STANLEY PALACE on the left, a lovely 'black and white' building which houses the War Services Women's Club. (This was restored in the mid 1930s and was (and is) the office of the English-Speaking Union). You know they often hold dances here and service women use the place to relax, meet friends and have tea. Stanley Palace has changed little and is open to the public on weekdays from 10.00am to 5.00pm apart from lunch times and Thursdays.

Down the hill from Stanley Palace beside the Watergate you will find the ROODEE, Chester's racecourse. There is no racing here these days - it has stopped until the war ends - and the racecourse buildings are now used for other purposes. There is an ordnance store there and part of the stables has been converted to house ATS girls!

*The Heinkel shot down over Chester, 14 August 1940. (Manchester Evening News, courtesy of Chester Chronicle).*

As you stand on the city walls now above the racecourse looking out across the Dee, you recall the newspaper report which told of an aerial battle here in August 1940 between three Spitfire training instructors from RAF Hawarden and a Heinkel III German bomber. The Heinkel was shot down and crashed in a field at Bumpers Lane, Sealand. You remember reading that a farmer and a local Home Guardsman took the five crew members prisoner and gave them tea at the farm.

*Airborne trolley made by Dixon-Bate, Chester.*

Turn left now and walk along Nuns Road towards the river. As you pass CHESTER CASTLE, the HQ of Western Command, which was responsible for all aspects of defence and training in the North West, see how well guarded it is and just look at all the sandbags around the building! You have heard there are some new buildings across the river in Queens Park which were hurriedly commissioned in September 1938 during the Munich crisis. There was no official opening, though, because that emergency hastened the move and forced total concentration on preparations for the now seemingly inevitable war. You can just about see the Queens Park complex with its protective bunkers across the river from the Groves as you pass. (The Castle's parade ground now serves as a car park for County Hall but in those wartime years it was regularly the scene of ceremonial parades and inspections - Princess Mary, the Princess Royal, visited Western Command on more than one occasion and inspected troops and ATS contingents here.)

The CHESHIRE MILITARY MUSEUM at Chester Castle is well worth a visit for it has displays on the history of all the local regiments, including items on the Second World War, like the pens used for signing the Japanese instrument of surrender in 1945. The Museum is open daily from 9am to 5pm all year round. Telephone Chester (01244) 327617 for more information. It is worth remembering here that there were a number of training camps located around Chester at the Dale, Upton and at Saighton, where new facilities were built at the beginning of the war. The 'local' regiments of regular and reserve troops were of course mobilised immediately war broke out and left the county within the first few days of September. The militia, the Cheshire Yeomanry, spent most of the war in the Middle East, protecting vital oil supplies. A cavalry regiment, the Yeomanry has the distinction of being the last British regiment to actually fight on horseback, in Syria in 1941. Later they were sent to Europe and the Far East.

Now you can enjoy a stroll along the riverbank and maybe stop to watch the sculls and canoes on the Dee. Then why not visit GROSVENOR PARK nearby, a favourite place with Cestrians for a Sunday afternoon walk, before you return to the station and catch your train back to camp.

You can see by standing in our serviceman's or woman's shoes that there was an enormous variety of entertainment in Chester. Its pubs and cinemas were always full of service personnel - British, Polish and later American. This was obviously very good for business but it often caused problems. There were many complaints about disorderly houses and the abuse of hotel rooms during the war which no doubt shocked respectable folk and there were several prosecutions.

Unfortunately it seems that there was a lack of facilities for service people who did not enjoy the livelier forms of entertainment too. For those who just wanted to relax away from camp life it was easy to feel lonely in a crowd. Local churches played their part, though, welcoming newcomers, many of whom brought letters of introduction from their own churches back home. The Queen Street canteen where men could get a cup of tea and a cigarette was popular, and the Army also built a new hut (near the Roman Amphitheatre) with the co-operation of the YMCA. It offered recreation for younger soldiers who would have otherwise been at a loose end, homesick and lonely. The British Restaurant in Northgate Street was for general use and you could get a reasonably priced meal there (charges were fixed and meals eaten here saved on rations). Children were banned from the restaurant though, unless accompanied by an adult as there had been many incidents of bad behaviour!

But don't think that Chester's war efforts were solely confined to shopping and entertainment. The working population of the city increased from 5,000 to 16,000 during this time which kept the Ministry of Labour and National Service Employment Exchange pretty busy. Many of those now registered for work during the national emergency were women who would normally have been at home. The Vickers aircraft factory at Broughton was a major employer and there were many smaller engineering works in the area. Perhaps one of the most interesting was the firm Dixon-Bate in Tarvin Road which manufactured aircraft parts and developed and made special airborne trolleys used by the parachute forces to provide transport after the Arnhem landing and in Normandy. These trolleys were used to carry ammunition and stores, and as stretchers for the wounded.

*Trolley unfolded.*

Although Chester was fortunate to escape severe bomb damage, there were several incidents which caused the loss of property and of lives. Happily there was no major destruction. As a result the city we see today is essentially the same as when our service friend visited it on leave some forty years ago. Re-development and new road construction have brought changes, of course, but Chester's character has little altered. It remains a city with much to offer the visitor.

---

**OTHER PLACES TO VISIT**

▶ *Grosvenor Museum.*
   Tel: 01244 321616

▶ *Chester Heritage Centre*
   Tel: 01244 317948

▶ *"On the Air"- Broadcasting Museum*
   *(Wartime aircraft and ships' radios on display)* Tel:01244 348468

▶ *Dewa Roman Experience*
   Tel: 01244 343407

▶ *Chester Candle Shop*
   Tel: 012444 346011

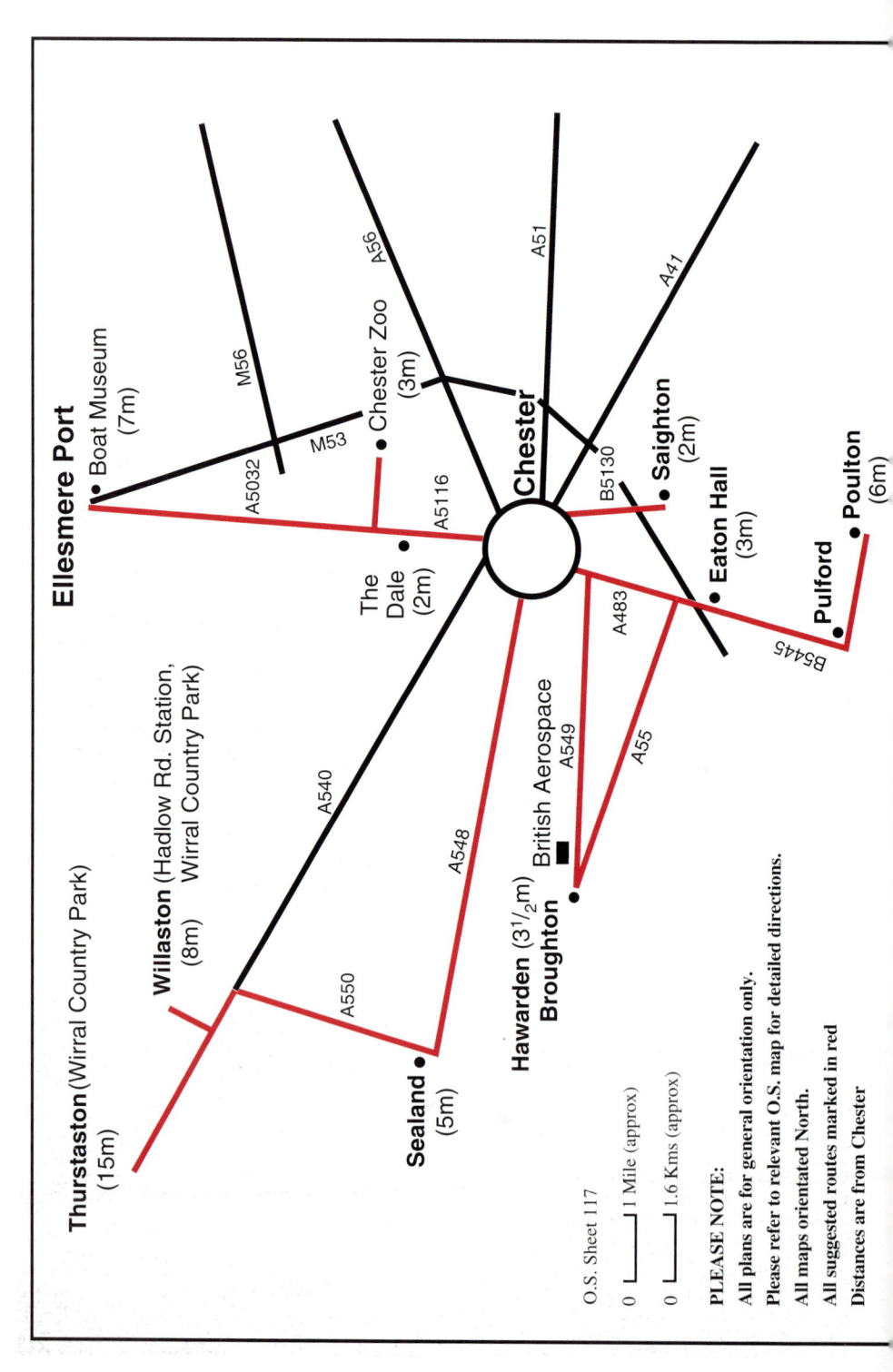

**Ellesmere Port**
- Boat Museum (7m)
- Chester Zoo (3m)
- Saighton (2m)
- Eaton Hall (3m)
- Poulton (6m)
- Pulford
- The Dale (2m)
- Thurstaston (Wirral Country Park) (15m)
- Willaston (Hadlow Rd. Station, Wirral Country Park) (8m)
- Sealand (5m)
- Hawarden (3½m)
- Broughton
- British Aerospace

Roads: M56, M53, A5032, A5116, A56, A51, A41, B5130, A483, B5445, A540, A548, A550, A549, A55

O.S. Sheet 117

0 ⊢⊣ 1 Mile (approx)
0 ⊢⊣ 1.6 Kms (approx)

**PLEASE NOTE:**
All plans are for general orientation only.
Please refer to relevant O.S. map for detailed directions.
All maps orientated North.
All suggested routes marked in red
Distances are from Chester

# An ABC of the Chester area

## *Animals, Boats and Camps*

Within easy driving distance of Chester's city centre you can visit a variety of places which have unexpected connections with World War II.

Let's take the Liverpool Road out of Chester (A5116) which leads through the suburb of Upton, and make for CHESTER ZOO. On the way, look out for the entrance to the DALE which is approximately two miles out and on the left. During the war, the Dale was a centre for the retraining of servicemen unfit for duty through illness or injury. Here they were well cared for until they were fit enough to resume their normal duties. Moston Military Hospital was also situated here. The Dale is still MOD property so is **not open to the public.**

Continue along the A5116 and turn right onto the A41 for the now world-famous Chester Zoo. During wartime, the danger of closure loomed large. It was difficult to obtain food for the animals there - remember that the sort of food some creatures needed just was not readily available - and if takings dropped, then the Zoo could not afford the upkeep. Enterprising management, however, launched a scheme early in the war whereby members of the public could 'adopt' animals by donating set sums for their upkeep. The scale of charges varied according to the size and eating habits of the animal concerned - a lion, for instance would cost 14s.6d a week while 40 monkeys could be fed for 1s.0d!

*Aerial view of the Dale in wartime. (Imperial War Museum).*

*Chester Zoo.*

Another scheme to help funds was the concessionary ticket offered to members of the armed forces in uniform and to evacuees. This, of course, made the Zoo very attractive to servicemen and women on short leave passes from nearby camps.

The public, too, responded well to appeals for materials for the maintenance of the Zoo - such as wire - and donated food. There were problems, however, when keepers were called up to the forces, and the aquarium had to close because of lack of staff. There was considerable anxiety at the time about the effects of air raids on the animals, and special precautions were taken. Public shelters were, of course, available and staff were trained to deal with emergencies like escaping animals. Luckily no such escapes occurred and the animals seem to have been relatively undisturbed by the noise. In fact, the only casualties the Zoo suffered during the war because of air raids were the fish in the lake. As well as its own stock of animals, the zoo became a home for other animals evacuated from the country's other zoos and circuses - many of these, such as Molly the Elephant quickly became additional attractions there.

In spite of all these difficulties, the zoo kept going. Even lack of public transport, which reduced the number of visitors, did not prevent it from showing a small profit, thanks to the loyal 'adopters' and the introduction of new ideas such as refreshments for visitors.

Chester Zoo is now open daily (except Christmas Day) and for more details on opening hours, you can telephone Chester (01244) 380280. Incidentally, you can still 'adopt' an animal!

Just across from the bus turning circle by the old north entrance to the zoo, you will find Acres Lane, Upton. In those days, a gun emplacement for H25 Heavy Anti Aircraft Battery was positioned here, manned by a regular unit of Royal Artillery and specially trained members of the local Home Guard. Part of the Home Guard training for this task took place on the range at New Brighton and also included a night time trip to Tatton Park near Knutsford (see page 63) to watch a parachute drop. This must have made the men even more conscious of the importance of their work. When not on duty at the gunsite, Home Guardsmen in this area might be on cycle patrol on the main road, or guarding bridges and crossroads in the lanes around Chester - a monotonous routine which must have been exasperating as well as tiring.

Let's return now to the A41. Look for signs to ELLESMERE PORT, and drive via either the A5032 or M53. Where the roads intersect (behind Junction 9 of the M53), you will find the BOAT MUSEUM which stands beside the Manchester Ship Canal. In the former Pattern Shop, the Museum has a local history display on Ellesmere Port which includes some interesting wartime material. The Wolverhampton Corrugated Iron Company and Burnells works both produced sheet metal here - including the corrugated iron used in making Anderson Air-raid shelters. With its important oil terminal, and the oil industry's new development centre at the Thornton Research Centre (Shell Oil), Ellesmere Port played a vital role in keeping the country's fuel needs satisfied. It was the point of origin of PLUTO (PipeLine Under The Ocean) which was essential in maintaining fuel supplies for the Allied invasion of Normandy.

The Boat Museum is devoted to the history of the inland waterways. It has many interesting exhibits to see and you can also wander at will around the dock area. The Museum does a great deal of restoration work on engines and boats and offers a fascinating day out. Open all year round except Thursdays and Fridays in winter. Refreshments are available and most areas are accessible to disabled visitors. For more details, telephone 0151 355 1057.

Further along the M53 towards Birkenhead (near Junction 6) is the site of HOOTON PARK AIRFIELD - part of which is covered today by Vauxhall Motor Car Works. Hooton Park had a varied history during World War II. It served first as a base for Coastal Patrol Aircraft (No. 3 CPF), whose task was to spot U-Boats and warn of any danger of attack from the sea. This was replaced by the School of General Reconnaissance, then by an Anti Aircraft Calibration Unit (which enabled AckAck units to check their accuracy by providing practice targets). Later No. 11 Radio School was based here. Some aircraft construction was also carried out - mainly by Martin Hearn Ltd., who hangars once stood on the south eastern section of the airfield. The Hooton Park aerodrome is being restored by the Griffin Trust who began running a programme of guided tours round the site in March 1995. For further details of tours and the Trust's work ring 0151 350 2598.

To the north west of Chester on the A550 lies RAF SEALAND. An already established base, Sealand became a hive of activity once war had been declared and pilot training was carried out with increased urgency. Many Battle of Britain

*Sheet Rolling Mills, Ellesmere Port. (Boat Museum, Ellesmere Port).*

pilots won their wings here. Amongst them were many Americans who volunteered for service before the USA joined the war.

After an attack on Sealand, which killed several airmen, a stray Heinkel III was tackled and brought down by Spitfires from RAF Hawarden. (See page 14). The plane had most probably mistaken the airfield for the Vickers factory across the river. In addition to training, Sealand also provided facilities for aircraft maintenance and repairs to Wellington and Lancaster bombers as well as Mosquitoes.

Now drive three miles north on the A550 and turn left on to the A540. Take a right turn 2$^1$/$_2$ miles further on which leads on to the B5151 to Willaston, at the southern end of the WIRRAL COUNTRY PARK.

This Park has been created along a 12 mile stretch of disused railway which once formed part of the Hooton to West Kirby line. If you wish you can park and picnic at the restored HADLOW ROAD STATION much as it was during the war. This railway line was used during the war for the transport of RAF personnel to and from West Kirby where initial training took place.

Further up the Park at THURSTASTON (off the A540 to the left and about 18 miles from Chester) the VISITOR CENTRE stands beside the former H28 Anti-Aircraft gun site, part of Liverpool's defensive ring. Those large landscaped mounds in front of the visitor centre cover concrete gun emplacements which once looked out across the river. What a commanding view the gun crews had of the estuary, a navigational focus for German bomber pilots. On the caravan site nearby, look for a wooden hut which once housed the gun crews on duty. Today this is a wash house for the caravan site. In those days, off-duty crews were accommodated on part of the Lever holiday camp.

The Wirral Country Park is accessible at various points along its length so there is no need to walk the whole 12 miles! For further information, you can telephone 0151 648 4371. The Thurstaston Visitor

*Former gun emplacements at Thurstaston.*

At **Parkgate Station Picnic Site**, also part of Wirral Country Park, a wartime concrete pillbox can still be seen in the old station yard. Pillboxes like this were erected at strategic points such as bridges and crossroads, to give cover to soldiers or Home Guardsmen defending the area if invasion came.

Centre is open from 10am to 5pm all year round.

**To the south and west of Chester you can find sites which were used by all three armed services. Unfortunately these are not open to the public, but you can include them in a pleasant afternoon's drive into the countryside.**

The first is SAIGHTON CAMP and to reach it you need to take the B5130 out of the city for approximately two miles. You will find Saighton on the left hand side. The Camp was built during the early war years and it is interesting to note that the construction of the camp was dogged by labour disputes. These were mainly about inadequate lodgings and allowances, but were unusual for a time when everyone was 'pulling together'. It was here that thousands of new recruits were trained and local people will remember the tramp, tramp, tramp of marching feet when soldiers went out on endurance training. It could often take an hour for a column of men to pass through a village!

Saighton had all the usual facilities of a large camp. Its theatre had regular shows put on by ENSA but most men based there (such as the golfer Henry Longhurst) will recall that camp life was often bleak and lonely.

Saighton had all the usual facilities of a large camp. Its theatre had regular shows put on by ENSA but most men based there (such as the golfer Henry Longhurst) will recall that camp life was often bleak and lonely.

Next on our journey we travel 5 miles south west of Chester leaving the city on the A483 (the main Chester - Wrexham road), turning left at the first roundabout after the A55 on to the B5445. After a mile, you will pass the gates and the long drive to EATON HALL on the left. Today this estate is the PRIVATE residence of the Duke of Westminster but in the war years his predecessor made the Hall available to the Army as a military hospital, retaining only part of it for his own use. The Hall, Chapel and its stables became a convalescent home for the Army and later were taken over by the Royal Naval College 'Dartmouth'. The Hall returned to private use in 1960 and a modern mansion has since been built on the site.

*Eaton Hall was used as a military convalescent home. (Chester Chronicle).*

If you go two miles further south to Pulford - also on the Eaton Estate - you will reach POULTON airfield. This acted as a satellite to Hawarden airfield and was used mainly for fighter training. Most of the buildings have long since gone, but you can still see the airstrip. This is also PRIVATE land and not open to the public.

From Pulford, return now to the B5445 then the A55. Turn west towards Wales here for $3^1/_2$ miles and take the exit for BROUGHTON. In the village you will find BRITISH AEROSPACE on the site of the original Vickers-Armstrong 'shadow factory'. During the war, 5540 Wellington bombers were produced here and from 1943 the factory also made Lancasters and a few Lincolns. To meet the imposed targets, workers would often have to put in a seven day week with little time off for relaxation. Those workers not on shift also had to do nightly firewatching duty. However, as the war drew to a close and thoughts were turning to the reconstruction ahead, part of this factory was turned over to the design and manufacture of prefabricated housing. This was to provide much needed accommodation for the homeless in badly bombed areas. These 'aluminium houses', complete with their 'aluminium kitchens' aroused much local interest when displayed at the Chester gas showroom!

Adjacent to the British Aerospace Factory you will find HAWARDEN AIRPORT, formerly an RAF station. Used mainly for pilot training, in common with most airfields, it also had a large maintenance unit. Hawarden was to become the temporary base for units such as the AACU (Anti Aircraft Calibration Unit) and the Air Transport Auxilliary Ferry Pool, whose pilots flew completed aircraft from here to the main RAF bomber bases in the south and East Anglia. Although not officially an operational unit, the flying instructors were nevertheless prepared to 'have a go' when enemy aircraft were spotted in the area. When their Battle Flight went into action in August 1940, a Heinkel was successfully brought down near Chester, (page 14) and again a Junkers 88 in the following September.

Not far from Broughton, Chester's Home Guard often held summer camps in the grounds of Hawarden Castle.

Although the camps were used for serious training, the men no doubt enjoyed the pleasant surroundings. They certainly enjoyed some good food and declared the cooking 'first rate'!

---

*OTHER PLACES TO VISIT*

▶ *Grosvenor Garden Centre, near Chester Tel: 01244 682856*
▶ *Gordale Garden Centre, Burton, Wirral Tel: 0151 336 2116*
▶ *Ness Gardens, Neston, Wirral Tel: 0151 353 0123*
▶ *Port Sunlight Village - Heritage Centre and Lady Lever Art Gallery Tel: 0151 644 6466*

---

The King and Queen visit 'a North Wales aircraft factory'. (Liverpool Daily Post, courtesy of Chester Chronicle).

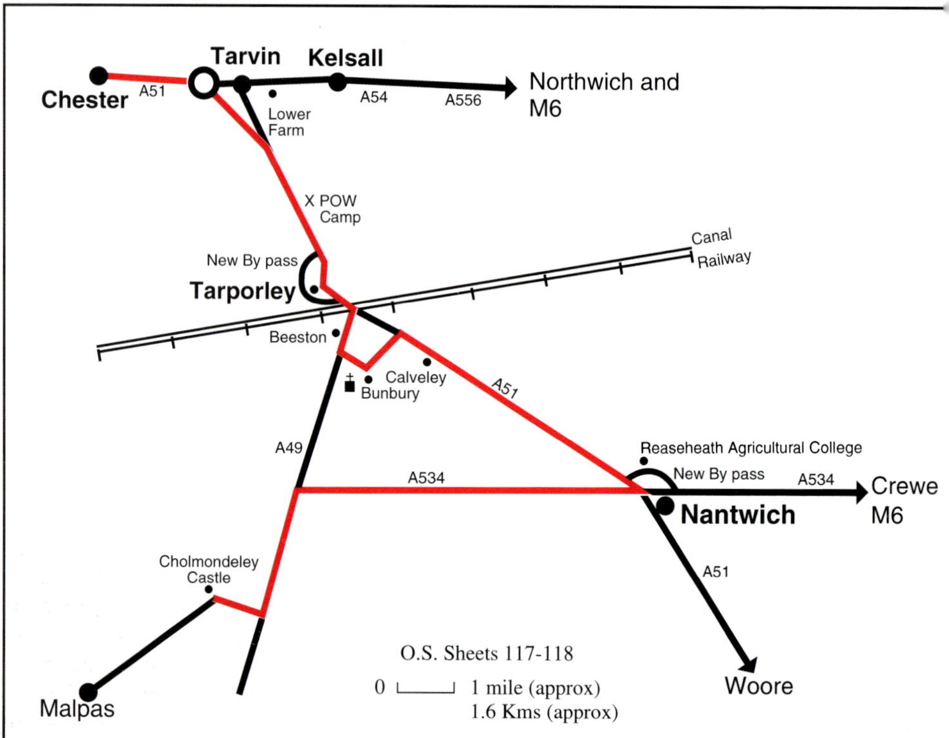
Tarvin
Kelsall
Chester
A51
Lower Farm
A54
A556
Northwich and M6
X POW Camp
Canal
Railway
New By pass
Tarporley
Beeston
Calveley
Bunbury
A51
A49
Reaseheath Agricultural College
New By pass
A534
A534
Crewe M6
Nantwich
A51
Cholmondeley Castle
O.S. Sheets 117-118
0 1 mile (approx)
1.6 Kms (approx)
Woore
Malpas

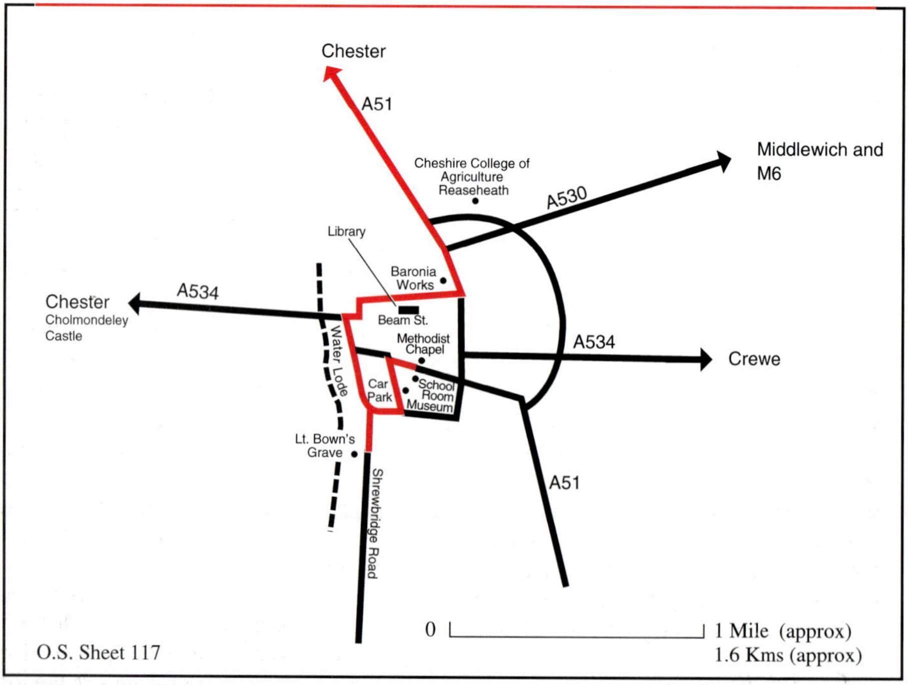
Chester
A51
Cheshire College of Agriculture Reaseheath
Middlewich and M6
A530
Library
Baronia Works
Chester
Cholmondeley Castle
A534
Beam St.
Methodist Chapel
A534
Crewe
Water Lode
Car Park
School Room Museum
Lt. Bown's Grave
Shrewbridge Road
A51
0 1 Mile (approx)
1.6 Kms (approx)
O.S. Sheet 117

# The Nantwich District

## Agriculture and Evacuees

This area south-east of Chester, characterised by its rural tranquillity, played a surprisingly active role in the last war. Its farms, market towns and small villages, all made a vital contribution to the war effort. Primarily an agricultural area, its farmers were under pressure from the War Agricultural Executive Committee to produce the required quantities of milk, crops and livestock. As a result of its neutral zone status, the area had also to cope with an influx of evacuees from the Channel Islands and Liverpool, as well as airmen and army personnel based on some of the larger estates.

Drive out of Chester on the A51 and make for the roundabout at Tarvin. Turn right. Had you gone straight on you would have passed on the right Street Farm, Kelsall. Its near neighbour, Lower Farm, distinguished itself during the war by being the farthest west landing point for a German flying bomb. It was on Christmas Eve 1944, shortly after 6am when the V-1 fell in a nearby field. Fortunately, no-one was injured. It was one of several directed towards Manchester in the last German terror campaign against the civilian population - the only occasion on which such a raid was attempted against the North West.

Nowadays there is little to remind us of this particular event in the peaceful countryside so after turning right at the Tarvin roundabout head down the A51 in the direction of Tarporley. Nearly a mile beyond the village of Clotton, a group of warehouse buildings comes into view on the left. Situated on what was once the Tarporley Racecourse, it was here that Italian prisoners were held during the war; the buildings were later used for Government food storage.

Continue now towards Tarporley and turn right onto the bypass skirting the town. Turn right again at the first traffic lights and follow the A49 to BEESTON. Coming down the hill here you will notice some large tanks set into the hillside behind the railway line. During the war these were used for fuel storage as they were conveniently placed next to the railway sidings. To take a closer look, turn sharp right immediately after passing under the railway bridge - see the sidings to the right next to the large Beeston Smithfield market.

Beeston was no stranger to war. A few centuries earlier its castle overlooking the Cheshire Plain was of local significance in the English Civil War. If you have time, visit the castle - for the active, the view from the top of castle rock is magnificent. Try to imagine the army units of the last war, their soldiers laden with equipment, training on the nearby hills or on route marches in the country lanes.

The next place on our journey is BUNBURY so turn left off the A49 and you will find the village about one mile south of Beeston. Bunbury is one of the most attractive villages in Cheshire and it is difficult to imagine its peace shattered by a severe air raid in November 1940 which destroyed a number of houses and caused serious damage to its 14th century church. Much of the church's glass was broken and the roof sustained extensive damage which though now repaired is still in need of attention. This lovely church contains some interesting exhibits, and unusual features such as Renaissance panelling and is well worth a visit if you have time.

Back on the road again now, let's leave Bunbury and make for ALPRAHAM by the road leading north east and rejoin the A51. As you pass through the countryside, remember the many evacuees from Liverpool billeted around here. According to one report at the time they were transformed 'from ragamuffins to

*Bunbury Church.*

what they ought to be... and it was a pleasure to the mothers of Alpraham to do it'. One wonders how such a patronising - if well-meaning attitude was received by the evacuees and their parents!

Next, follow the A51 south to WARDLE, just south of Calvely, for two miles. On the right, next to North West Farmers' dairy and the radio telescope (positioned at the base of a wartime hangar), Green Lane leads you to an industrial estate. This is accommodated in the buildings which once served Calvely

*Freedom for evacuees to play in the Cheshire countryside.*

*Calvely airfield.*

Airfield. Old hangars, Nissen huts and blockhouses remain in various states of repair. There is an air of desolation here but the surviving buildings give a clear impression of the airfield of old. The main runways are on private land to the north of Wardle Hall and were built in 1941. Originally planned as a fighter base, the shifting priorities of wartime meant that the station was used almost exclusively for training fighter pilots. You can still see the network of roadways and hard-standing for parked aircraft. Having served its purpose admirably, Calvely was abandoned in 1946.

Leaving the airfield now, let's head south on the A51 towards Nantwich. Just north of the town is the CHESHIRE COLLEGE OF AGRICULTURE at Reaseheath. The war had forced the closure of standard training courses but Reaseheath was to provide an unusual service. It was here that some 1,200 Land Girls were trained in the skills of poultry keeping, animal husbandry and arable farming. Then they were sent out to help farmers whose regular farmhands had joined the forces. Farmers were extremely hard-pressed during those wartime years. Labour shortages coupled with increasing

*Land Girls. (Harris and Price, Liverpool).*

demands for more food for the nation, plus the inconvenience of double summer time and land requisitions, all contributed to this. The Women's Land Army was formed to help farmers use the pool of female labour mobilised during the war. Though most girls preferred factory work or the Forces, the Land Girls found their work tough but rewarding. Farmers were sometimes hostile to women workers - especially those who were well meaning but ignorant of farming ways. Those who were properly trained at Reaseheath, however, were capable workers who could be sure of appreciation. Normally, the college is not open to the public but it does hold an Open Day in May. For details telephone Nantwich (01270) 625131.

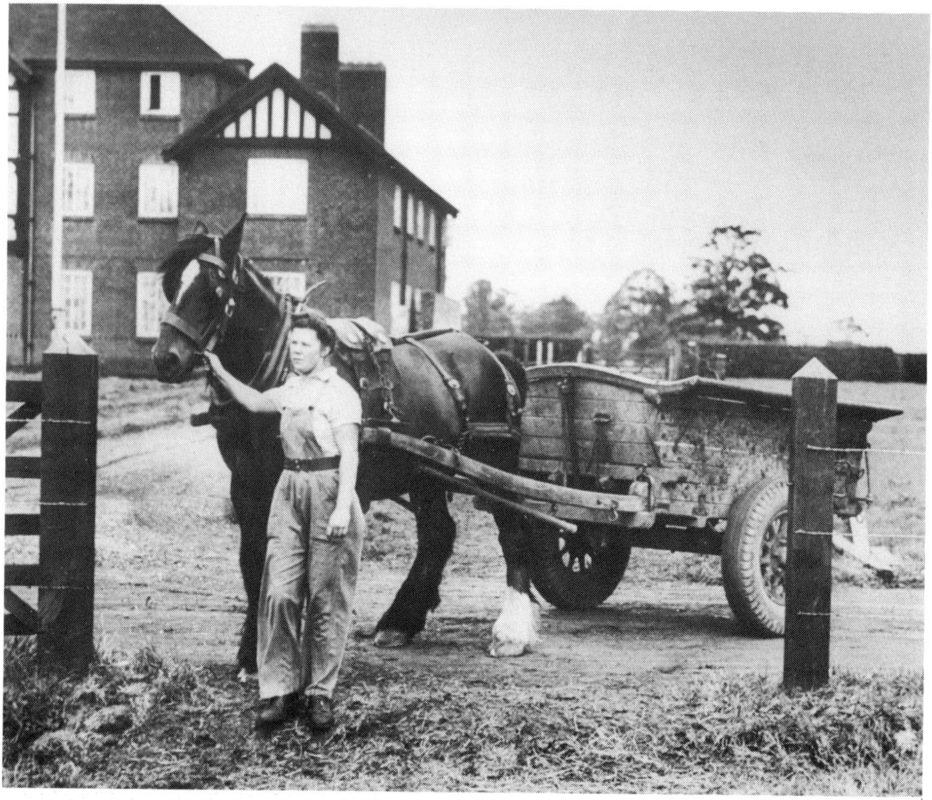

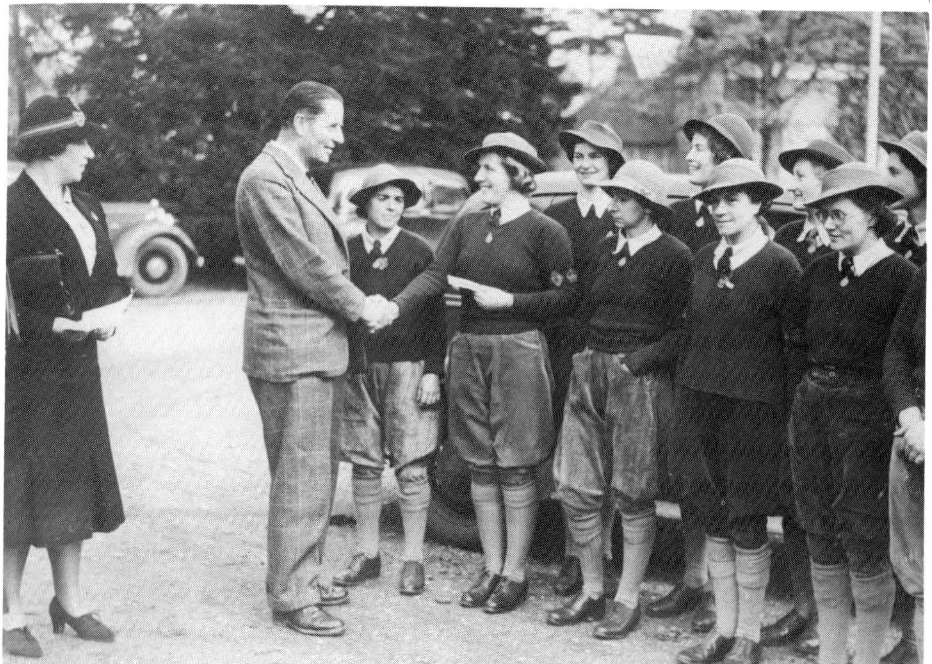

If you continue into Nantwich on the A51 you will pass the red brick Baronia Works of John Harding & Sons, clothing manufacturers, on the right opposite Barony Park. Here production was turned over to the supply of army uniforms and later 'demob' suits issued to all servicemen at the close of the war. Now turn right at the traffic lights into Beam Street, then follow the one-way system to traffic lights before the river where you turn left along Water Lode and left again into the car park adjoining Pillory Street.

From here you can begin a pleasant stroll around the town. First, why not visit the NANTWICH MUSEUM in Pillory Street which has a collection of local material, including some Second World War exhibits which are featured periodically. The Museum is open Mondays to Saturdays from 10.30am to 4.30pm. For further details 'phone (01270) 627104.

Walking northwards now along Pillory Street, turn right into Hospital Street. A short way ahead you will see the 18th Century Methodist Church on the left and opposite on the right, the Methodist Schoolroom. Here the WVS ran a forces canteen and on Saturdays evacuees from Guernsey would meet regularly during their long stay in the area. The Channel Islanders and local people struck up long lasting friendships and today many still return to visit their temporary 'homes' and 'families'.

Let's return along Hospital Street and cross into Mill Street to walk across Water Lode to visit the memorial to Nantwich's Great Fire. Look for a path just beyond this spot which leads off to the right. Follow the path for nearly half a mile to find the well cared for GRAVE of Lieutenant Leslie Brown, USAAF. This grave marks the place where Lt. Brown crashed his Thunderbolt in January 1944. He deliberately remained at the controls of the plane when it developed engine trouble on a flight from nearby Hack Green. His actions in steering the aircraft away from a densely populated area before it finally crashed earned him the respect and gratitude of the people of the town. His grave at the rear of the

*Methodist Schoolroom, Nantwich.*

*Grave of Lt. L. Brown, Nantwich.*

houses in Shrewbridge Road serves as a poignant reminder of those lost as a result of war away from the battle front. You can also drive to Shrewbridge Road where you will find another access point to the riverside walk.

Now, back to the car and on to our next stop at CHOLMONDELEY CASTLE some 13 miles west of Nantwich via the A534 and A49. Here a variety of 'guests' were housed during the war years - children from Liverpool during the war's early months, followed by the Pioneer Corps and then the Royal Engineers and finally it was used as a Naval psychiatric hospital. In those days the Castle was known as 'Cholmondeley I' and the stables and domestic quarters as 'Cholmondeley II'.

In common with other large estates Cholmondeley had its own Red Cross detachment, Air Raid Wardens and Auxilliary Fire Service. Many Land Girls helped the farmers and anti-aircraft units were active nearby.

Happily the castle itself suffered little war damage - even during the night of 28 November 1940 when virtually the whole of Western Cheshire was affected by a severe air raid. A land mine did fall in the grounds at Sicily Oak Farm causing such a severe blast that most of the 16th Century glass in the Ancient Chapel was shattered. However, fragments were carefully collected and labelled for reinstatement. This painstaking task was only completed in 1954, using similar glass, from the Castle, to supplement that from the Chapel itself.

Shortly after Dunkirk, you might have seen Polish troops encamped in the Park or the Czech troops who were to stay here for almost six months. These men had escaped from Occupied Europe after Dunkirk.

During their stay here the Czechs made many good friends in the area but eventually they were reorganised and sent off on training courses and defence patrols in other parts of the country. Several VIPs visited the camp including President Benes and Foreign Minister Jan Masaryk of the Czech Government in exile.

*Czech soldiers relaxing, Cholmondeley Park, 1940.*

Airmen, however, remained here for a short time only. The shortage of pilots in the summer of 1940 meant they were urgently needed for active service. Many displayed great courage in the Battle of Britain and later operations, and others were recruited by the Special Operations Executive, trained and then parachuted into enemy territory on secret missions.

There was one sour note however. Some of the Czech forces had Communist sympathies and declared their lack of support for the war when Molotov, the Soviet Minister, congratulated Von Ribbentrop on Germany's success. They were immediately separated from the main Czech contingent and were not included in the preparations to fight Germany until Russia entered the war.

Cholmondeley Castle Gardens are open (afternoons) on Sundays and Bank Holidays from Easter to October and Wednesdays and Thursdays, May to October. For more details, 'phone 01829 720383.

*President Benes visiting Czech troops, Cholmondeley Park.*

> **OTHER PLACES TO VISIT:**
> ▶ *Stapeley Water Gardens, nr. Nantwich. The 'Yesteryear Collection' includes wartime memorabilia such as a Churchill Tank and Jeep.*
> Tel: *01270 628628*
> ▶ *Bridgemere Garden World, south of Nantwich Tel: 01270 520381*
> ▶ *Bunbury Watermill, Bunbury 01270 665667*
> ▶ *Cheshire Candle Workshops, Burwardsley. Tel: 01829 770401*
> ▶ *Snugbury's Ice Cream Farm, north of Nantwich Tel: 01270 624830*
> ▶ *Peckforton Castle, near Beeston Tel: 01829 260930*
> ▶ *The Firs Pottery, Aston, Nantwich Tel: 01270 780345*
> ▶ *Cheshire Ice Cream Farm, Tattenhall Tel: 01829 70995*
> ▶ *Country World, Tattenhall. Dried flower workshop, animal paddock Tel: 01829 71070*
> ▶ *Stretton Watermill, near Farndon Tel: 01606 41331*

*Czech Memorial in Cholmondeley Park, sculpted by Frantisek Belsky.*

32

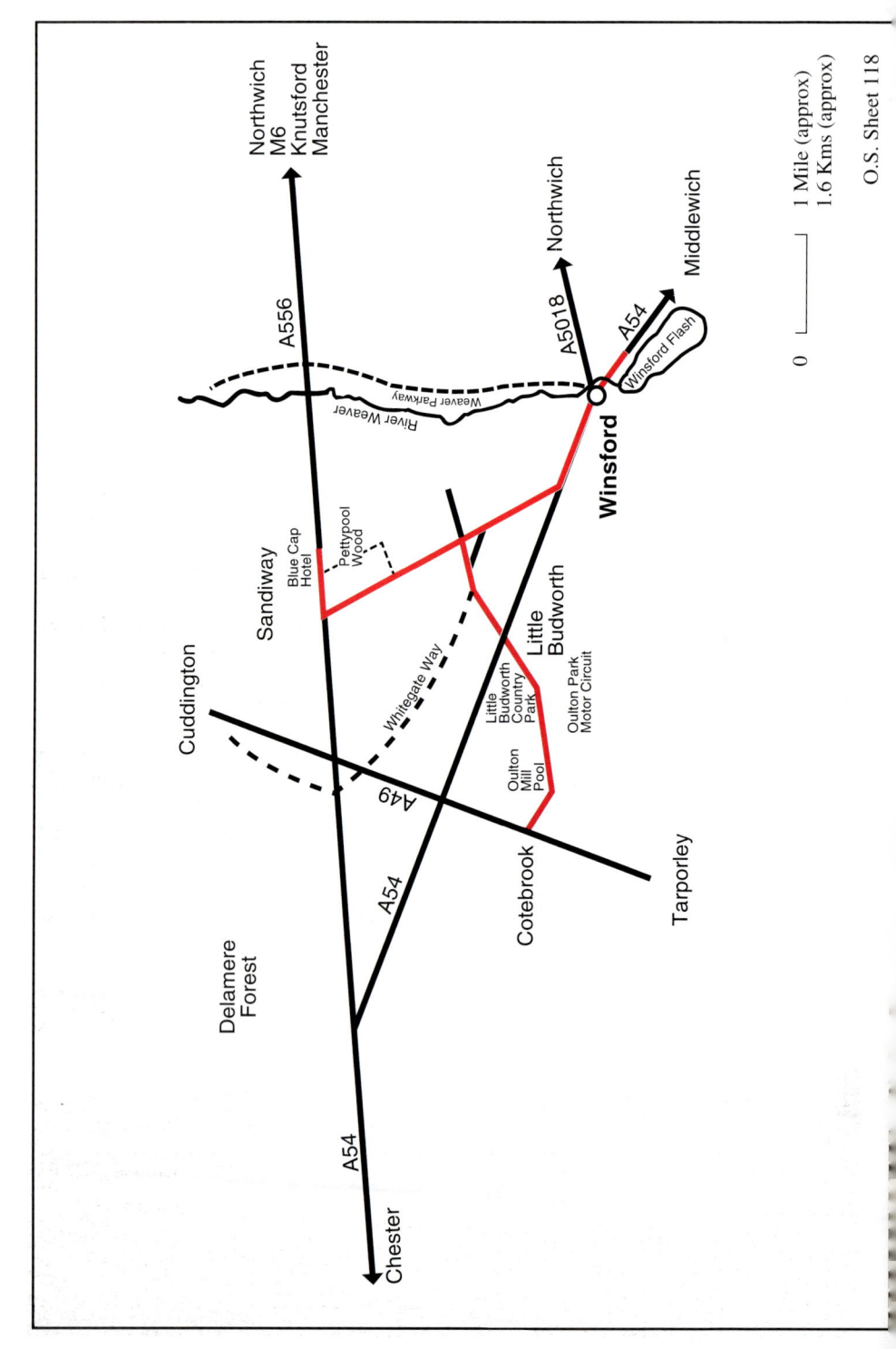

# Vale Royal

## *Tanks, Troops and a Night of Terror*

In the heartland of Cheshire lies Vale Royal which derives its name from the abbey founded by Kind Edward I and Queen Eleanor in the 13th century. Still largely unspoiled by housing and industrial development even today, throughout the war it offered an ideal location for training troops.

One of the main salt producing towns of Cheshire, WINSFORD, can be found in this area. From here, salt and other goods were taken to NORTHWICH on the River Weaver, and then by canal to the chemical works at Runcorn and Widnes which used salt in their production.

Let's begin at the western side of Vale Royal. Start by turning off the A54/A556 on to the A49 south and make for the village of COTEBROOK. Turn left in the village onto a minor road which brings you to OULTON MILL POOL, a beautiful spot where you can park and picnic if you wish. It is hard now to imagine the peace of this lovely place being disrupted by enemy raiders, but in November 1940, on the night of the 'big raid', it suffered a severe attack - unusual for a place so far away from normal bombing targets.

Local people were well used to hearing the drone of Luftwaffe bombers overhead each night on their way to Liverpool, but on 28 November the bombers turned back and shed their load of bombs over a strip of countryside running roughly south east from Ellesmere Port to Nantwich. This was

*Oulton Mill Pool.*

the night when Barrowmore Hospital, Bunbury Church and Cholmondeley Castle were all hit (see pages 6 and 30)

The incendiary bombs which fell all around Cotebrook and Little Budworth started several fires, and landmines gouged craters in the ground. One man, driving in the dark, failed to see one such hole in the road at Cotebrook. The result was that his van nose-dived into the crater which was so deep that he could not climb out! Local people recall the sky bright with the fires started by the incendiaries and how the planes' searchlights lit up the ground! One family even spent the night in the open air, sleeping in a sand-hole for protection. The German planes were flying so low that they could strafe the ground with machine-gun fire. It certainly was a night to remember.

Next turn left at the Mill Pool and after driving for half a mile you will come to LITTLE BUDWORTH COUNTRY PARK which has parking off the road. This is opposite the entrance gates of OULTON PARK, Cheshire's motor racing circuit. The area offers an interesting walk through woods and heath on what, in wartime, was a troop training zone.

*Little Budworth.*

At the onset of war, Oulton Park became a military camp. It was to accommodate an astonishing variety of troops including French and Polish as well as British. Later came the Americans and Canadians. At first they were housed in tents, then in the autumn of 1940 (shortly before the big air raid) wooden huts were erected

Much of the Park and Common was requisitioned for military use. The War Agricultural Committee was also involved here, decreeing what crops should be produced on the rest of the estate. One estate worker recalls how the deer in the Park had to be prevented from damaging crops in the newly planted areas and how, when they had just completed a sunken fence to confine the animals, the 'War Ag' sent word that the deer should be shot. "Lady Grey Egerton, out in her invalid chair, shouted at the men in an attempt to prevent this, but nearly all the deer were killed then or later on," he reminisced. "It was a terrible thing." There was no room for compromise with the War Ag and farmers had to obey their instructions or risk dispossession. They also stipulated that twelve cows should be kept on the estate and a certain amount of feed was allocated for this, but it meant a lot of extra work when labour was scarce and the estate was short-staffed.

Sometimes the military presence caused problems and resentment. Budworth Common lost all its trees to make way for tank training for General Patton's troops - hardly popular with the residents of that pretty place.

There was of course the absurd side of life. Many soldiers were total strangers to the countryside and so found the night-time sounds quite unnerving. There is a story which tells of a night when camp guards at Oulton heard footsteps approaching in the adjoining field. Their challenges went unanswered in the darkness and the footsteps continued. Finally the sentry fired in their direction. He subsequently discovered - to his acute embarrassment - that he had shot Old Charlie, one of a pair of horses which had been walking quietly along beside the hedge in their field.

Oulton Park is not generally open to the public - unless there is a motor racing event taking place, but Little Budworth Country Park and Oulton Mill Pool are always open and worth a visit. Both provide a good opportunity to savour the peace of Cheshire's countryside.

Let's leave Little Budworth and head for the WHITEGATE WAY. Passing Budworth Pool on the left, drive for approximately one and a quarter miles to reach a crossroads with the A49. Go straight across this and continue on the minor road following signs for the Whitegate Way, a country trail created along the track of a disused railway line.

Car parking is available at the old station here and if you walk eastwards for a few hundred yards, you will come to a gate and waymarker. Look directly across from here and you will see a field and the backs of a group of houses.

The large house you see to the left is called Cassia Lodge and this was used for billeting troops, including some survivors of Dunkirk. They were brought here straight from the boats which carried them safely home. There was no time to let their families know where they were, and the caretaker at the Lodge had no prior warning of their arrival. He had to organise everything at a moment's notice and then go and buy stamps for the soldiers to send messages to their families.

Later, when the Americans used the Lodge, additional facilities were needed. Two large wooden huts were erected in the garden at the rear of the house. The field was occasionally used by light aircraft - presumably for officers - and General Patton is said to have visited his men here. The Americans who were billeted at Whitegate were friendly and popular with the locals.

The GI's stationed at Whitegate were preparing for the Normandy landings and the tanks they used in training were concealed nearby. Most training took place in Pettypool Wood close at hand where assault courses were conducted and there the troops practiced crossing rivers and climbing nets and rope ladders. There are several public footpaths leading into the Wood and you can reach these by turning left at the crossroads a quarter of a mile from Whitegate Station and heading towards the A556. There is an access point to the Wood roughly halfway along this road and another footpath from the A556 just opposite the Blue Cap Hotel in Sandiway.

Alternatively, you can turn right at the Whitegate crossroads and drive for about two miles into WINSFORD. Many parts of the town reflect its 19th century industrial history. The generosity of local salt magnates is clearly visible. Look for example at the red brick public buildings

*Whitegate Station*

*Winsford Flash.*

to the left of the dual carriageway which skirts the modern town centre and leads down the hill to a large roundabout. Take the third exit (Middlewich Road) and you will find a car park on the right beside a stretch of water known as the Winsford Flash. Now used for watersports, the Flash was the scene of a huge celebratory bonfire on VE Day.

The River Weaver, which runs through the town, ensured Winsford's industrial success in the 19th century. It was of course an important artery of communication. Its banks were lined with warehouses laden with goods awaiting shipment. Nowadays it is possible to walk from Winsford to New Bridge (about 1$^1$/$_2$ miles) and then to follow the towpath to Northwich. This walk is known as the Weaver Parkway and begins near the large roundabout almost directly opposite the Winsford Flash, beside the Red Lion Pub. The patway leads off behind the pub.

The inland waterways of Cheshire were still an important means of transport in the Second World War and the canals and rivers were carefully maintained to ensure the smooth flow of traffic. The Weaver at Winsford flows north to link up with the Trent and Mersey Canal at the ANDERTON BOAT LIFT near Winnington, Northwich, an important connection between the natural and artificial waterways of Cheshire and the first boat lift in the world. The lift is being restored to full working order and there is a floating Visitor Centre on the canal adjacent to it. Telephone 01606 862862 ext 3322 for further information.

**OTHER PLACES TO VISIT:**

▶ *Cheshire Herbs (A49, $^1$/$_2$ mile north of A54 junction) Tel: 01829 760 578*

38

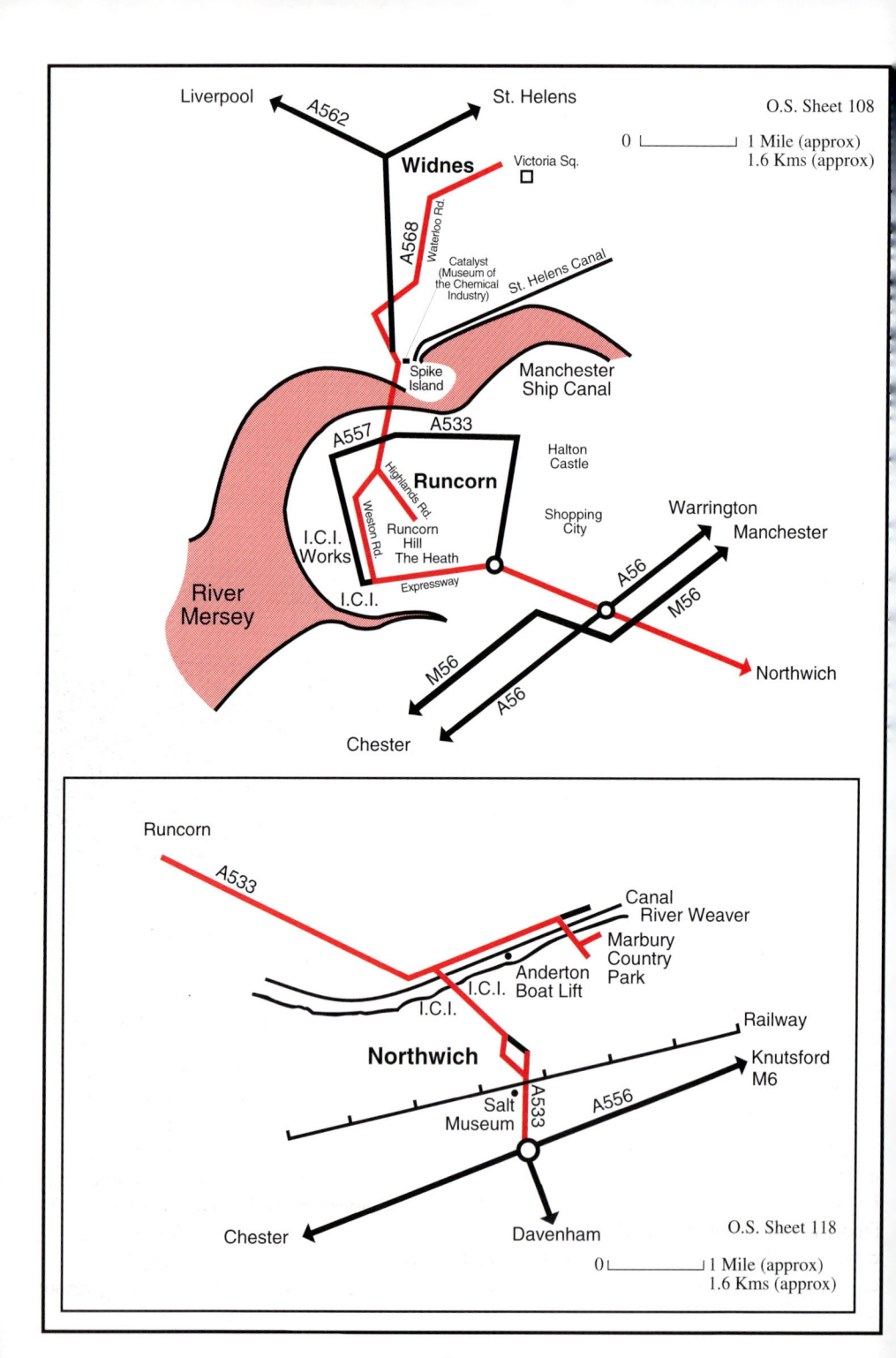

# Northwich - Runcorn - Widnes

## *Chemicals in Wartime*

The importance of salt to Cheshire's industrial development has been mentioned previously, and the central area of the county engaged in salt production contains a great industrial heritage. It also forms the backbone of the chemical industry in the North West for salt is a vital ingredient of many chemical processes.

The 19th century brought many changes to the ancient tradition of salt production. The towns of Northwich, Runcorn and Widnes with their good communications and transport links became the pulse of this thriving, modern industry. Firms such as Castner-Kellner, Brunner-Mond (ICI) and Albright and Wilson, amongst others, set up plants which used brine and rock salt in their production processes and began to manufacture chlorine, ammonia and soda ash. These products were used in the manufacture of bleach, glass, paper and soap - all industries which can still be found in the North West.

As the 'wich' in Northwich tells us, the town in centred in an area rich in rock salt and brine beds. This meant it naturally developed close links with the chemical industry, which became a major employer in the area. It is our first port of call. And what better place to start than the town's SALT MUSEUM.

*The Salt Museum, Northwich.*

The Salt Museum is signed from the roundabout at Davenham on the A556. Incidentally in the weeks before D-Day camouflaged tanks and armoured vehicles were stockpiled here along what is now the A556 Northwich-Knutsford road as part of the massive secret preparations for the Allied invasion of Europe. The Museum was once a Workhouse and you will see it on the left about one and a half miles from the roundabout. Here you will find displays and information about the development of the salt industry in Cheshire from its beginnings to the present day including wartime.

Then, POWs were drafted in to supplement local labour, which was in short supply. The Museum is open Tuesday-Saturday and Bank Holidays. Telephone Northwich (01606) 41331.

*A salt-works outing, shortly after the war. The group includes German prisoners who would soon be repatriated.*

Let's leave the Salt Museum now and turn left. If you continue on towards the centre of the town you will see signs for Runcorn on the A533. Drive one and a half miles further and from the top of a hill you can look down at the immense ICI plants at WINNINGTON and WALLERSCOTE. From this vantage point it is easy to see how the chemical industry has dominated Northwich since the days of Brunner-Mond.

Like so many other industries, the chemical industry was making ready for the war that was to come. Even before 1939 it was responding to government requests for co-operation. No-one wanted the war but it was best to be prepared for the worst. British industry had been unprepared for the Great War and its leaders were determined not to make the same mistake twice. On the outbreak of war, an immediate increase in production would begin. New products of potential military value were urgently researched and factories and their staff were trained to cope with the dangers an air raid would pose - including fire drills, anti-gas drills and first aid.

ICI had a variety of chemical plants around Northwich, ranging from brine pumping operations to soda ash production. It is impossible to go into

*I.C.I. Works, Winnington (I.C.I.).*

*I.C.I. plant at Wallerscote (I.C.I.).*

great detail here but two sections do deserve to be singled out for their particular contribution to the war effort.

First, let's look at the development of a new material - polythene - which is now part of our daily lives. It was during an experiment that an interesting 'waxy solid' was unexpectedly produced in 1933. ICI soon saw its potential as a substitute for rubber, and although at first it was difficult to produce in large quantities, they went ahead with the construction of a pilot plant at Wallerscote in 1939. Polythene soon proved to have ideal qualities for electrical insulation in high frequency radio transmitters and receivers. Thus its use in Britain's Radar equipment (which gave accurate information on imminent Luftwaffe air strikes) was invaluable to the defence of the country.

Commenting on the value of this new material, Sir Robert Watson-Watt, FRS, said, "The availability of polythene transformed the design, production and installation problems of airborne Radar from the almost insoluble to the comfortably manageable".

Not far from the polythene plant, part of ICI's research division at Winnington - code-named 'Tube Alloys' - was hard at work on the development of the atom bomb. While other companies were involved in different aspects of its design and development, 'Tube Alloys" main task was to separate the uranium isotope U235 from the more common isotope U238. This was achieved by using uranium hexafluoride gas in a diffusion process. This was a difficult project and it has largely gone unrecognised because of secrecy, political disagreements and the ultimate application of the rival American research into the manufacture of the first A bombs.

If the Luftwaffe had succeeded in hitting ICI's Northwich Works, it would have had disastrous results in terms of the war effort - not to mention severe casualties. Fortunately, their raids on the area did not bring any major boost to Nazi morale. However, bombs did fall in the vicinity of Northwich on many occasions. ICI employees adhered to strict security and safety codes and also attended air raid and (poison) gas drills. During the latter, tear gas was actually pumped into the air raid shelters - not a pleasant experience for those who forgot their gas masks. (Anti-gas drills were routine in factories, schools and offices, since it was always considered possible that Germany would resort to using poison gas against the civilian population.)

The next stop on our tour is MARBURY COUNTRY PARK. To reach this, drive down the hill between the ICI plants until you come to a narrow bridge over the River Weaver and the Trent & Mersey Canal. Turn right after this towards Comberbach and drive for just over a mile. Look out on your right for the Anderton Lift mentioned in detail on page 37. The Country Park is off the main road to the right. Today this is a leisure area, with walks, and birdwatching

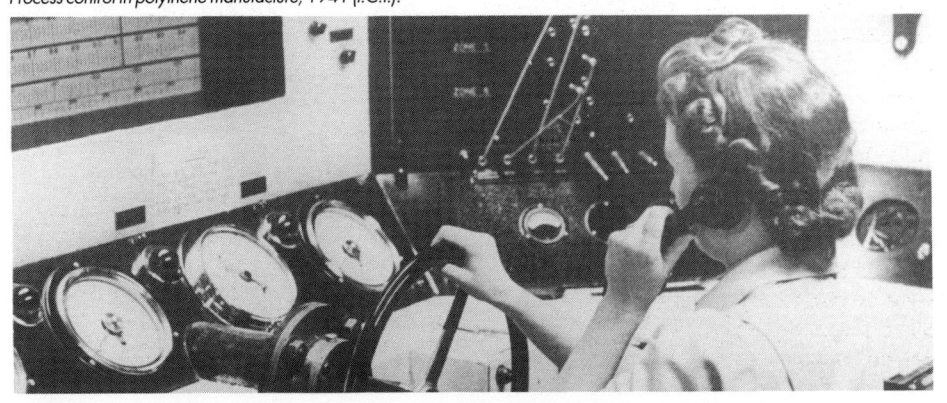

*Process control in polythene manufacture, 1941 (I.C.I.).*

on Budworth Mere. The Park was once a private estate surrounding Marbury Hall, a mansion built in the style of a French chateau. At the outbreak of war, the Park and Hall were requisitioned by the War Office. A number of Dunkirk survivors were brought here by bus from Northwich station. An eye-witness recalls that they looked dejected and exhausted, dirty and unshaven - and very young.

*Marbury Hall in Wartime. (Note the American truck).*

The Park was later to provide accommodation for an assortment of troops - including the Americans - and wooden huts were built along the avenue of lime trees. The Hall itself was used as an administration centre. The building has since been demolished for it became unsafe. Traces of it still remain today and you can still see some of the steps and paths of its garden. The wooden huts have disappeared, too, but stand in front of the Ranger's office and you will see the line of the lime tree avenue where they once stood.

Local people remember the Americans based at Marbury (and at nearby Wincham Hall) as a friendly and outgoing lot, although they soon noticed the rigid separation of white and coloured soldiers, even on social occasions. The Americans were very sociable and often arranged dances and concerts for the locals.

Everyone enjoyed being entertained by the GIs, who treated their visitors to the almost forgotten luxuries of chocolate cake, real coffee and, for the ladies - nylons!

There were so many American troops in the area that a 'Donut Dugout' (a canteen providing American food) was opened in Northwich by the WVS.

Towards the end of the war, Marbury's wooden huts housed German prisoners of war. Many of them were classified as incorrigible Nazis - although the basis for this seems doubtful in some cases. Gradually, contact with the local people increased and the prisoners were able to go out walking and visiting nearby families. Some prisoners went out to work in the salt works and to ICI's soda ash plant. This was not always popular with the employees there. Prisoners were thought to be too privileged, particularly when their concert party played in public, but by 1947, when POWs were being sent home, relations were generally good.

During those years there were also a number of Polish refugees occupying another part of the Park, near the kitchen garden.

Marbury Country Park is open to visitors during daylight hours, all year round. Telephone Northwich (01606) 77741 for details. The park rangers will be pleased to answer any questions.

Let's return now to the main road and follow the A533 for roughly 8 miles in the direction of RUNCORN. Runcorn is a mixture of old and new. The old town lies to the west, with its docks and chemical works, while to the east is the modern Shopping City. This is only a short distance from Halton Castle and the ancient Seneschal's House. In this century - particularly in World War II - Runcorn's chemical industry has made an immense contribution to our national economy - indeed to national survival. We go along the modern Expressway now towards Weston Point where the heart of Runcorn's chemical industry lies. You can take this road right to Runcorn Bridge but perhaps a better view can be found if you turn off the Expressway towards The Heath. Then turning left into Cavendish Farm Road leading into Weston Road, you will find several good spots to look down at the vast Rocksavage and Castner-Kellner works.

*German P.O.W.'s sketch of the huts at Marbury. (Courtesy of E. Hatton).*

Castner-Kellner, part of ICI's General Chemicals Division, produced chlorine and various derivatives here during the war. These made a vital contribution to many areas of the war effort from simple hygiene to the development of polyvinyl chloride (PVC) as a substitute for virtually unobtainable natural rubber, and cyclohexanol, an ingredient of the fibre of the future - nylon. Other chemicals produced here were used in the manufacture of fertilisers and armaments, and included tetra-ethyl lead, a fuel additive which improved the performance

*Chemical works in Runcorn.*

of aero engines. Like so many others, this works had its own Home Guard unit and made the astonishing contribution of over £200,000 to National Savings.

The nearby Rocksavage Works, part of Mond Division (ICI), produced phosgene and chlorine - also important for camp hygiene - and derivatives including refrigerants, anti-freeze compounds and ingredients for DDT and anti-malarial compounds.

It is not possible here to give full details of all the chemical companies in existence in this area at the time, but Albright and Wilson of Widnes do deserve special mention. This company manufactured phosphorus which was used in munitions, flares and in agriculture. Their products also included Molotov Cocktails and some devices intended to set the Black Forest in Germany alight. (However, these proved unsuccessful in practice).

Now you have a good idea of the size of the chemical works on the Runcorn side of the river, turn right out of Weston Road and right again into Highlands Road. There you will find a road on the right which leads to Runcorn Hill - another spot overlooking the River Mersey and the Manchester Ship Canal. In the hillside here were tunnels used as air raid shelters, and possibly for storing munitions. The marks on the rock where a searchlight once stood are visible. The Mersey Estuary was protected by a number of Ack Ack batteries, several of which were close to Runcorn, at Sutton Weaver, Preston Brook and Moore. (Incidentally Violette Szabo, the courageous secret agent, was stationed at Sutton Weaver before she joined the Special Operations Executive - see also page 74.) Runcorn and Widnes are only some 10 miles from Liverpool and were uncomfortably close to some of the worst bombing of the war at Bootle and the Liverpool Docks.

Let's drive from here down into the old town and across the bridge to Widnes, on Queensway. The somewhat precarious-looking transporter bridge of old has been replaced by a more modern bridge but during the war the old bridge was a vital link between the two towns. Take the first exit once across the bridge and bear right into Waterloo Road then turn right into Mersey Road and you will find Spike Island on your left. The St Helens Canal meets the Mersey here so this was once an important junction for waterborne traffic and an area densely covered with chemical works such as Hutchinsons. Now all this has been developed as a leisure area and one of the buildings you can see - the Gossage Tower - once a soap factory - is now open to the public as Catalyst, the Museum of the Chemical Industry. There are many fascinating "hands-on" exhibits which tell the story of the heritage of the area including the war years and an observatory 100 feet above the River Mersey. Open Tuesday to Sundays and Bank Holiday Mondays 10am - 5pm. Telephone: 0151 420 1121.

*Widnes Transporter Bridge. (Catalyst, Museum of the Chemical Industry).*

Bomb damage at I.C.I. research laboratory. (Catalyst, Museum of the Chemical Industry).

Wartime workers in Widnes. (Catalyst, Museum of the Chemical Industry).

## OTHER PLACES TO VISIT:

- ▶ **Norton Priory Museum and Gardens, Runcorn Tel: 01928 569895**
- ▶ **Castle Park Arts Centre and Craft Workshops, Frodsham Tel: 01928 735832**
- ▶ **Lion Salt Works, Marston, Northwich Tel: 01606 41823**
- ▶ **Sutton Fields - Golf Driving Range, Crazy Golf, Walks, Pets Corner. Tel: 01928 791001**
- ▶ **Sovereign Cruises Ltd - cruises along the River Weaver. Tel: 01606 76204.**
- ▶ **Mouldsworth Motor Museum, near Frodsham. Tel: 01928 731781**
- ▶ **Halton miniature railway Tel: 01928 735832**

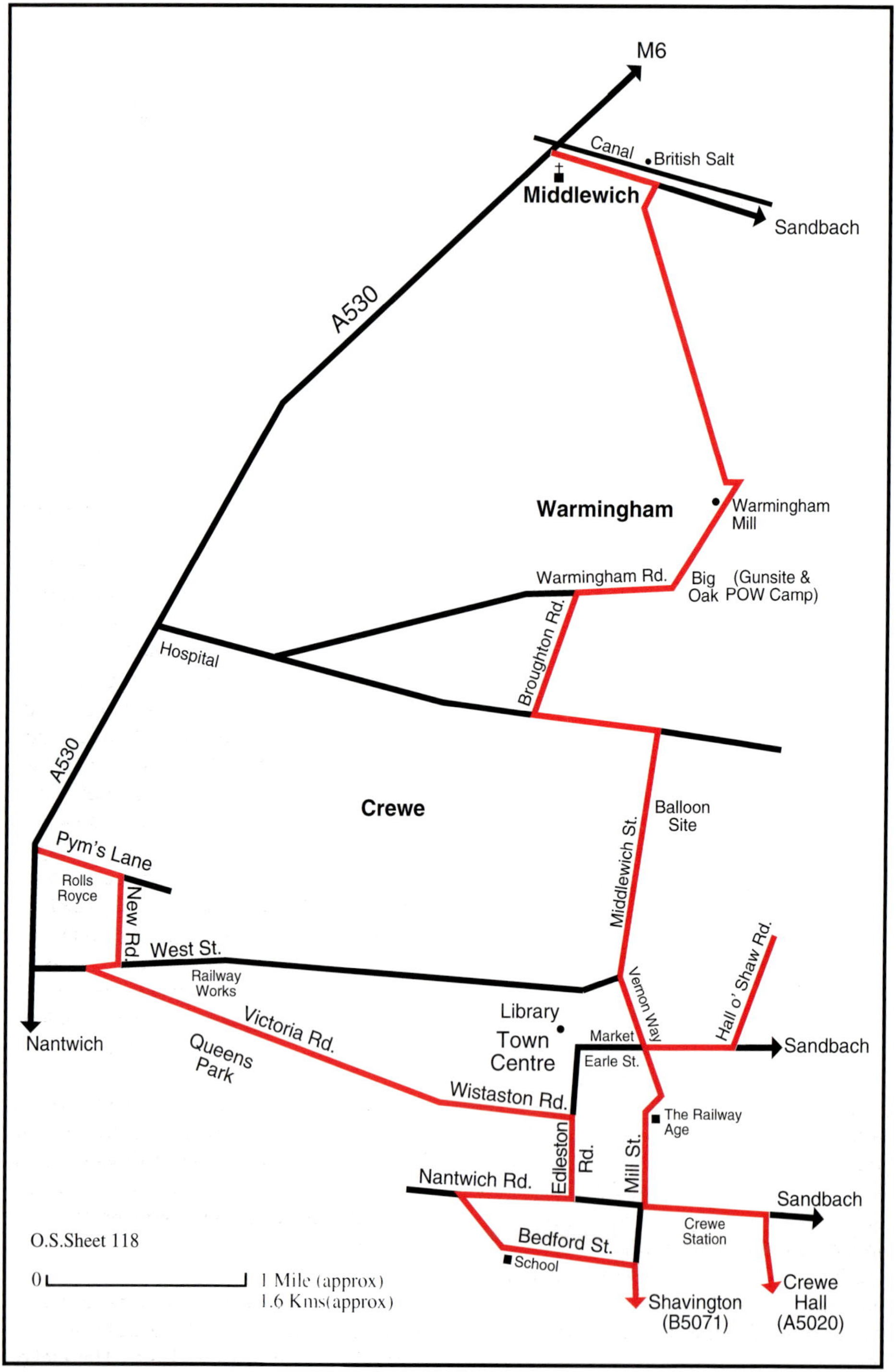
M6
Canal
British Salt
Middlewich
Sandbach
A530
Warmingham
Warmingham Mill
Warmingham Rd.
Big Oak
(Gunsite & POW Camp)
Broughton Rd.
Hospital
A530
Crewe
Balloon Site
Middlewich St.
Pym's Lane
Rolls Royce
New Rd.
West St.
Railway Works
Vernon Way
Hall o' Shaw Rd.
Nantwich
Victoria Rd.
Queens Park
Library
Town Centre
Market
Earle St.
Sandbach
Wistaston Rd.
The Railway Age
Edleston Rd.
Mill St.
Nantwich Rd.
Sandbach
Crewe Station
Bedford St.
School
Shavington (B5071)
Crewe Hall (A5020)
O.S.Sheet 118
0
1 Mile (approx)
1.6 Kms(approx)

# Crewe at War

## Smoke Screen and Balloon Barrage

When asked what Crewe means to them, many people will reply "changing trains", "missed connections" or perhaps "Rolls Royce". Amazingly all these instant associations are significant - then as now, for Crewe played a vital role in the war effort, and this made its defence against aerial attack essential.

The town had been a major railway junction since the 19th century and there were enormous railworks there. It was inevitable therefore, that Crewe would have a crucial role to play in the transport of goods and personnel and in the production and maintenance of the rolling stock needed to keep everything moving in wartime. The railway works was a major employer so Crewe already had a pool of skilled labour available. This was an important factor in the decision to site the Rolls Royce shadow aircraft engine factory on the outskirts of the town in 1938. At that time the Government was preparing to step up production in industries vital to the war effort, hence the setting up of 'shadow' factories to duplicate established production lines such as those of Rolls Royce at Derby or Vickers-Armstrong at Weybridge. As well as providing the capability to increase production, this system offered a safeguard against disaster should the parent company be seriously damaged or destroyed by air raids.

The presence of the railway and Rolls Royce made Crewe a target for enemy bombers. It already lay on the Luftwaffe flightpath to Liverpool, as pilots navigated by following railway lines and natural features such as rivers. The town had to have its own Ack Ack batteries, barrage balloon unit, and, in the early days, a smoke screen provided by the Pioneer Corps. The smoke screen was fairly effective but hardly popular with residents, for the small was appalling. Thick smoke was produced by lighting oily rags in the bottoms of numerous cylinders (a bit like dustbins) which were positioned along certain streets. These were kept burning for as long as necessary. Of course, on moonlit nights this was more important than ever and residents would rush to ensure not only that their blackout screens were in position but that there were no gaps round windows and doors to let the obnoxious smell into their houses!

It would be difficult to see all the places of wartime interest that Crewe has to offer. The best plan is probably to drive from one point to another, stopping when you feel like taking a closer look. Parking is relatively easy.

Let's start on the western side of the town and leave the A530 Middlewich-Nantwich Road at Pym's Lane. Here take a look at the outside of the Rolls Royce Works. Although you cannot look inside the works, you can see the original gatehouse on Pym's Lane which led to the shadow factory. Inside the works, many of the original fabrication shops are still in use though there has of course been much additional building since 1945.

The importance of the Rolls Royce Works in producing the legendary Merlin Engine can hardly be exaggerated. This engine with various modifications was used to power many different types of aircraft from Spitfires and Hurricane fighters to Lancaster bombers. More than 6000 Merlins and 2000 Griffon engines were produced here between 1940 and 1945.

*Workers in the shadow factory. (Rolls Royce).*

When you consider the difficulties which hampered production in the early stages, this achievement is all the more remarkable. Lack of accommodation for workers brought in from outside the area was a serious problem, but after much pressure, the local council hastily erected housing on the nearby Leighton Park estate. Local opinion was for a time outraged at the number of women doing men's jobs here, and being paid well for doing so.

The danger of air raids was every present. The factory buildings were camouflage-painted so that from the air they looked like a housing development. Even so, on 29 December 1940, the factory was hit. No. 16 shop was severely damaged with 18 people dead (mainly women) and some injured. In spite of this, work went on.

Turn right from Pym's Lane now into New Road which backs on to the Rolls Royce works. When you reach a junction at West Street, you will see the high walls of Crewe Railway works (now the premises of ABB Transportation). Behind these walls, everyone was working hard for victory during the war years. At this and the other rail works in Crewe at that time, skilled men were turning their hands to producing anything that was required - even tanks for the army.

Turn right now into West Street and take the second left into Victoria Road. Look for the playing fields on the right and QUEENS PARK, a leisure area of which Crewe is rightly proud. This was the wartime scene of many Home Guard drills and parades.

*Home Guard on parade at Queens Park.*

Let's continue on down Victoria Road and turn right into Edleston Road. Here turn right into Nantwich Road at the traffic lights then left into Bedford Street and on the corner of Bedford Street and St. Andrews Avenue, you will find the former Bedford Street School, a wartime First Aid Post. This area was the scene of severe damage. On 29 August 1940 some fifty houses were hit and the street was blocked with debris... the price of its proximity to Crewe Station.

Next we make for the village of Shavington-Cum-Gresty by turning right out of Bedford Street into Gresty Road (B5071). Here one mile outside Crewe, the CHESHIRE CHEESE pub earned the dubious distinction of being the first victim of air raid damage in Cheshire. Six high explosive bombs fell in the area on 29 July 1940 causing damage to the road and shattering windows over a one mile radius. Fortunately no-one was injured and the damage was only superficial.

Passing through Shavington, turn left on to the A500 and follow it for 2½ miles. Next turn left on to the A5020 and head back towards Crewe. Approximately two miles later you will see the magnificent mansion of CREWE HALL on your right. Crewe Hall belongs to the Duchy of Lancaster (the Queen's estate) and in 1939 was immediately offered to the nation.

Controversy raged in Crewe about this. Some people objected strongly to the original suggestions that it should be used to house evacuees on the grounds that "it was too good for those sort of people". Why, they would want pubs, cinemas and chip shops nearby! Then the Council came up with an alternative - it should be used as a military hospital.

Eventually the Hall was used to billet various regiments, the Royal Scots Fusiliers among them. Later it was handed over to the Americans and later still, it became a prisoner of war camp with German soldiers billeted in wooden huts. Camp 191's purpose was the re-education of its inmates, to convert them from their National Socialist values towards democratic ideals. When they were not attending lectures, prisoners spent their time performing theatricals, doing craftwork etc. to relieve the boredom and monotony of camp life. Crewe Hall is not open to the public but you can get a good view of it from the road.

*Crewe Hall Prison Camp amateur players. (K. Bock. courtesy of M. Kochan).*

*Crewe Hall Prison Camp. (E. Schormann, courtesy of M. Kochan).*

49

Approximately one and a half miles beyond Crewe Hall, turn left at the roundabout and head into Crewe. CREWE STATION stands on the left - a famous place and familiar to all wartime service personnel passing through the town in transit or on leave. Often the victim of complaint and criticism over delays, the railway played a vital role in keeping everything moving around the country. Road transport was not nearly as commonplace then as it is now so rail was the natural choice for the movement of heavy goods. The LMS staff were well prepared for the outbreak of war and had stockpiled essential equipment such as signalling gear. Thus air raids did not disrupt the railways too much and services were restored quickly. The volume of traffic - which of course the war increased dramatically - often caused delays - especially after an air raid. During air raids, the fires on steam engines had to be extinguished for safety reasons for the glow of the coals could be seen from above. Delays occurred simply because once the fire was out it took hours for the boilers to get up steam again.

Ammunition trains were sometimes 'parked' in sidings at Crewe - an obvious hazard which caused much anxiety to those living nearby.

The railways also had to cope with increased passenger traffic at this time. VIPs were touring the country to boost morale too. When the King and Queen travelled around the country by rail - as they frequently did - it called for special measures. A policeman was stationed on every bridge en route and all points had to be set and locked to prevent the risk of another train using the same section of track.

During those war years, the vaulted glass roof of Crewe Station was blacked out with thick paint and lighting at night was kept to a minimum. Troop trains were welcomed by volunteers armed with tea and sandwiches at all hours of the day and night. There was a Forces canteen not far from the Station in Nantwich Road, set up by the WVS. Run by a devoted team of volunteers working shifts, they gave a 24 hour service. Though most

*Barrage balloons over Crewe.*

*Bomb damage in Crewe.*

'customers' were only passing through, the local balloon barrage units and Pioneer Corps in charge of the smoke screen ate most meals there and a mobile canteen and shop serviced the balloon and Ack Ack sites in the area.

Continue our tour now by turning right at the roundabout into Mill Street, then right into Vernon Way which skirts the town centre. About a mile from the station you will reach a roundabout junction with Earle Street and here you will find the municipal buildings and market place just opposite the Law Courts. This was where Churchill's car was mobbed by an enthusiastic crowd of 7,000 people during his nationwide victory tour in the summer of 1945.

To the right and about a quarter of a mile up Earle Street (near the junction of Hall O'Shaw Road) the most serious civilian bombing incident in the Crewe area took place. Fourteen people were killed - including a policeman - and more than 30 injured.

Let's go along Vernon Way into Middlewich Street now. Just over halfway along on the right you can see some bungalows built on the site used by Balloon Command. There were 32 barrage balloons detailed to the Crewe area. (The danger of entanglement in their cables was a deterrent to pilots attacking targets in the area.)

Now let's turn left at the end of Middlewich Street, cross the roundabout and turn right into Broughton Road (just before the bridge over the railway line). About a quarter of a mile further, turn right at the junction into Warmingham Lane. An anti-aircraft battery once stood at Big Oak where the road bends to the left. One local resident remembers it well. He recalls they were naval guns and fired only once, sending furious puffs of smoke into the sky. Unfortunately, they had little effect on the enemy aircraft overhead! This site with its wooden huts later became a prisoner of war camp. The prisoners - mostly Italian and German - worked on nearby farms.

A mile and a half further on, why not stop and take a closer look at WARMINGHAM MILL, which is on the left, just beyond the Bear's Paw pub. Once an engineering workshop, during the war the Mill came under the control of MAP (Ministry of Aircraft Production) and produced aircraft parts - mainly wing jacks for Wellington bombers (made near Blackpool) and some hydraulic valves for Barracudas.

In 1939 the village was without electricity so a generator had to be provided to meet the Ministry's production targets, and a turbine house was built at the rear of the Mill in October 1940. There is a plaque set into the wall of the turbine house which is probably the earliest to commemorate the Battle of Britain. You can see this part of the Mill if you ask permission.

During the war, the roar of Merlin engines on test at the Rolls Royce works could be heard clearly here.

Appropriately a Merlin-Packard engine (made under licence in the USA) is on display at the Mill which now houses a number of individual craft units, including a wood turner, silversmith and ceramic workshop.

To meet demand, forty men were employed on both day and night shifts. When not at work, their spare time was taken up by Home Guard duty - even a tiny hamlet like this had to be ready to defend itself with road blocks etc.

Taking leave of Warmingham now, head towards MIDDLEWICH. Turn left at the T junction about one mile from the Mill and immediately right into Warmingham Lane, Middlewich. Next, turn right at the end of the lane and then left at the T junction with the main road. Here you can see, running parallel with the main road the Trent and Mersey Canal with British Salt's works behind. During the war, Middlewich was one of Cheshire's salt

*Warmingham Mill.*

# Memorial to courage

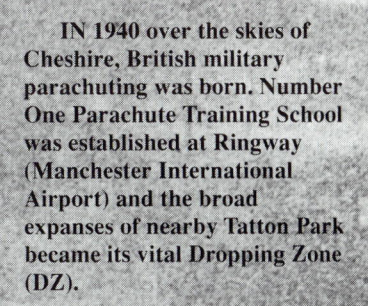

IN 1940 over the skies of Cheshire, British military parachuting was born. Number One Parachute Training School was established at Ringway (Manchester International Airport) and the broad expanses of nearby Tatton Park became its vital Dropping Zone (DZ).

Sixty thousand men and women: soldiers, SAS, special agents and resistance fighters of 14 nationalities and even dogs, pigeons and a 15 year old boy working for the French Maquis made 400,000 descents onto Tatton's soil or into the waters of Rostherne Mere between 1940 and 1945.

Here in pictures is the story of the courageous men and women who risked their lives in the days of pioneer parachuting and who contributed in a major way to the Allies' final victory.

### *Airborne Forces Memorial, Tatton Park*

*On the edge of the Dropping Zone is the simple memorial to "those who descended here in the course of training, given or received, for parachute service with the Allied Forces in every theatre of war." Fifty or so parachutists died at Tatton; it is chilling to remember that people jumped with only one parachute; there were no reserves as there are today.*

*The Memorial is on the* **Wartime Tatton Trail** *(see page 67)*

i

# GROUND TRAINING AT RINGWAY - INSURANCE AGAINST INJURY

Trainee parachutists underwent rigorous ground training at Ringway before the real thing. They were taught synthetic exits, control in the air, landing technique, PE to build strength, care and fitting of parachutes and getting out of the harness when being dragged across the ground. Only when the instructor was satisfied they were "fit to drop" did he let them move on to the next stage - dropping from balloons at Tatton.

*King George VI and Queen Elizabeth inspectin trainees at Ringway*

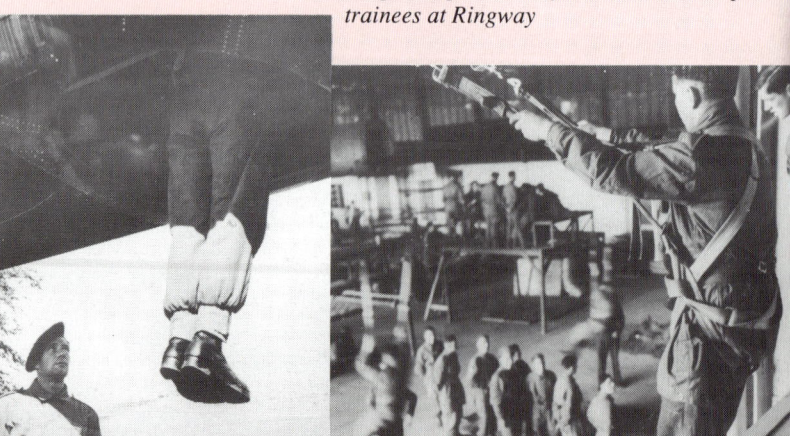

*Exiting from the aperture in a Whitley bomber needed a lot of practice: one could easily smash one's face against the metal of the aircraft and receive the dreaded "Whitley Kiss".*

ii

# JUMPING FROM BESSIE

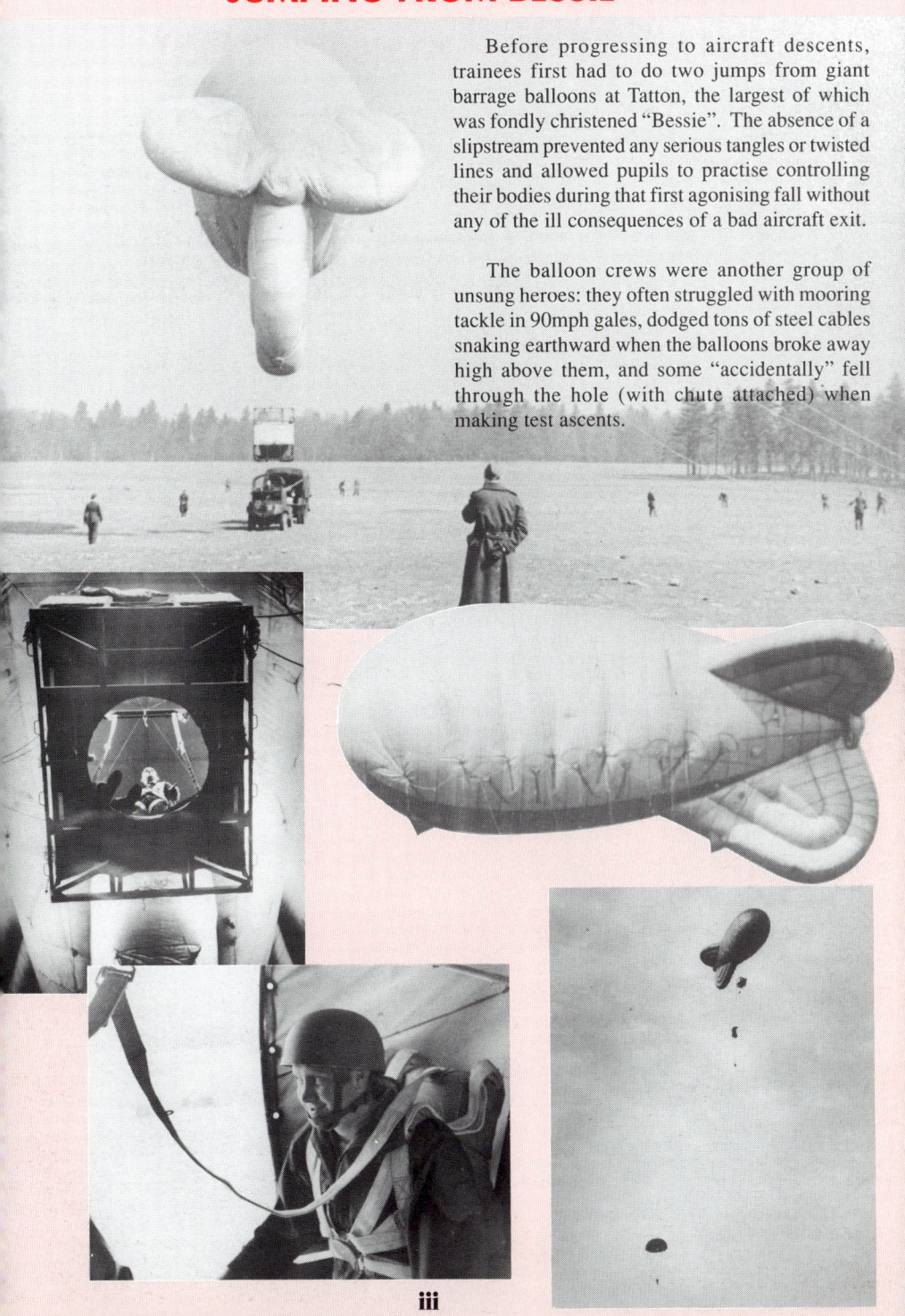

Before progressing to aircraft descents, trainees first had to do two jumps from giant barrage balloons at Tatton, the largest of which was fondly christened "Bessie". The absence of a slipstream prevented any serious tangles or twisted lines and allowed pupils to practise controlling their bodies during that first agonising fall without any of the ill consequences of a bad aircraft exit.

The balloon crews were another group of unsung heroes: they often struggled with mooring tackle in 90mph gales, dodged tons of steel cables snaking earthward when the balloons broke away high above them, and some "accidentally" fell through the hole (with chute attached) when making test ascents.

# AIRBORNE OVER CHESHIRE!

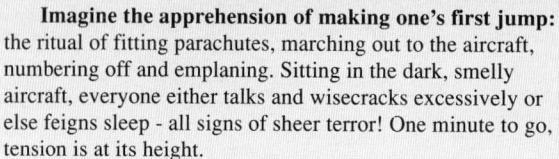

**Imagine the apprehension of making one's first jump:** the ritual of fitting parachutes, marching out to the aircraft, numbering off and emplaning. Sitting in the dark, smelly aircraft, everyone either talks and wisecracks excessively or else feigns sleep - all signs of sheer terror! One minute to go, tension is at its height.

"Red on, Green on. Go!" And the first man disappears through the aperture. Two seconds of agonising fall and buffeting in the slipstream and then the blissfull silent floating and the sudden panic when the earth rushes up at an alarming speed for the last few feet. Then the intoxicating relief and elation when one gets up still in one piece.

# AIRBORNE OVER CHESHIRE!

# THE HAZARDS OF TATTON
## - WIND, WATER, DEER AND TREES

Landing unintentionally in one of the ponds or meres in the area could have tragic consequences, and some drownings did occur. However, there were some amusing (in retrospect) incidents like the occasion when a soldier landed on a frozen lake. A strong wind was blowing and he became a human ice-breaker as his wind-filled chute ran away with him. Once safely back on dry land he muttered that he had made two important discoveries: one, ice was very sharp and two, his matrimonial prospects had been somewhat whittled away.

Nowadays, parachutists are taught tree-landing procedures but in the early days trees were a real problem and many a trainee had to be rescued by the Knutsford Fire Brigade. Much to his embarassment, one macho parachutist drifted into a tree on a particularly foggy night and hung there emitting Tarzanic cries of "HELP". When at last he was tracked down by his comrades he was non too politely informed that the distance between his heels and the ground was a mere 12 inches!

Tatton's deer herd, could be a hazard too. There is a tale about a soldier landing on the antlers of a none too docile stag. The stag lost a goodly part of his head gear, the parachutist all desire for wedlock, holy or otherwise.

# ALL PART OF THE TEAM

*A Whitley and a Dakota doing [D]rop.* Parachutists of yester year [wil]l always remember the fearful [res]ponsibility of the pilots and [na]vigators, who, day after day, no [ma]tter the weather, got their aged, [ov]er-worked aircraft off the ground [an]d delivered their nervous cargo [at t]he right height to the right place [at t]he right time.

*WAAF parachute packers at [Ri]ngway.* Throughout the war [ye]ars only one accident was traced [to] faulty packing. The pupils were [all]owed to see the women at work [an]d everyone had complete [co]nfidence in their skill. In fact, [on]e of the many army chaplains [wh]o trained here confessed: "Until [I s]at on the edge of the hole in the [ba]lloon, I had always put my trust [in] the Almighty. At that moment, [ho]wever, I'm afraid 90% of my [fai]th was in a WAAF packer!"

*The YMCA mobile canteen at Tatton.* Trainees remember with affection, the devoted ladies who supplied them with "cuppas" and refreshments at all hours of the day or night.

# SECRET AGENTS OF THE SPECIAL OPERATIONS EXECUTIVE

Ten thousand men and women trained to parachute under great secrecy as agents and saboteurs. Special instructors and aircraft would be allocated for them, since they were invariably in a frantic hurry. On occasions, a pupil would travel overnight to Ringway, do two hours of ground training, climb into a waiting truck and be whisked back from Tatton, draw another chute and repeat the performance, and by midnight he or she would be on the train for London ready to be dropped into enemy territory a few nights later.

The author Evelyn Waugh who wrote "Brideshead Revisited" and other well-known works was a special agent who trained at Tatton. He landed badly and broke his leg.

Odette - Resistance heroine who died aged 82 early in 1995. She was brutally tortured by the Gestapo and imprisoned in Ravensbruck concentration camp. In 1946 she received the George Cross for her bravery. She too, learned to parachute over Cheshire.

The story of parachuting and the many other events and activities which took place at Tatton Park is told in a 24 page booklet available price £1.00 from Tatton Park Gift Shop or for mail order details phone 01565 654822. The guide also takes the visitor on a walk round the park to the Airborne Forces Memorial and across the Drop Zone.

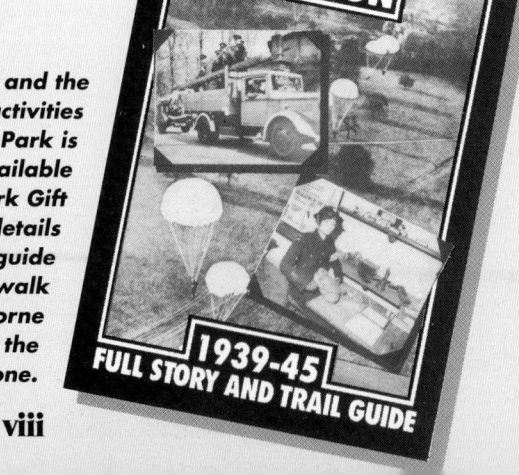

*Warmingham Home Guard.*

*Wellington wing jacks ready for despatch at Warmingham Mill.*

producing towns, linked to the chemical works on the Mersey by this canal and the Weaver Navigation.

Continue on into the centre of Middlewich. Beside the traffic lights stands the parish church. The shopping area is to the left of this. During the war, the vicar here was an Army Chaplain, and was captured at the time of Dunkirk. Released by Germany on health grounds, he returned home briefly, then retrained as an Airborne Padre with the newly formed parachute regiments. In this capacity, he took part in the disastrous landing at Arnhem, and was again taken prisoner, because he chose to remain with the wounded rather than take the chance to escape. This time he was to spend the rest of the war in a prison camp!

### OTHER PLACES TO VISIT

▶ *The Railway Age (Vernon Way) - Working signal boxes, steam and diesel engines. Miniature, model and standard gauge railways. Photographic displays of World War II events in Crewe. Tel: 01270 212130*

▶ *Museum of Primitive Methodism, Englesea Brook Tel: 01782 720289*

54

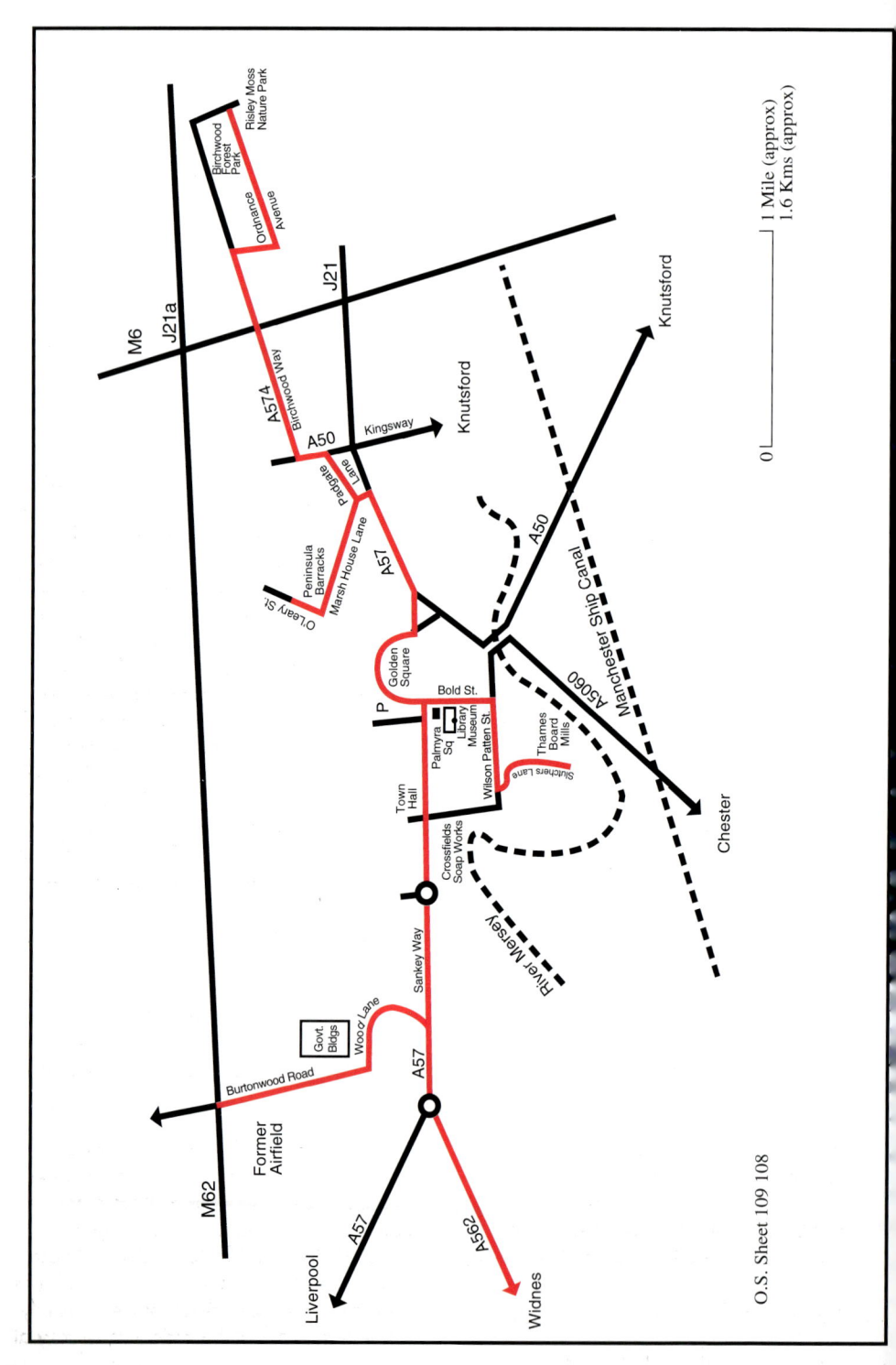

# Warrington

## *Arms, Airmen and Americans*

Warrington lies on the northern boundary of modern Cheshire. Today it is an important business centre, surrounded by new housing estates and industrial units. However, the heart of the town has remained intact in spite of progress and still retains the character of its late Victorian prosperity. Before the war years, Warrington was perhaps best known for its mills, tanneries, engineering works and its prime position beside the River Mersey and The Manchester Ship Canal. During the war, however, the town was to become the centre for two new wartime industries - munitions and aircraft production. Both of these were to make a significant impact on the life of the town and its people.

As you enter Warrington from the direction of Widnes on the A562 and join the A57 Liverpool Road approximately 1 mile from the town centre, you will see signposts for BURTONWOOD to the left. Anyone with an interest in aviation will have heard of Burtonwood and remember that during the war it was the centre of an enormous airfield complex, with construction and repair depots, where huge numbers of military personnel - mainly Americans - were housed. Follow the signs, first into Hood Lane and then right into Burtonwood Road to reach the camp.

It was in the early stages of the war that the site of Burtonwood was selected and developed. When it was realised that air supremacy was going to be a critical factor in eventual victory, resources were poured into the supply and maintenance of aircraft. Burtonwood was well located on the limits of enemy bombing range and close to the port of Liverpool. American co-operation was being anticipated even before the Lend Lease scheme was agreed and Liverpool was a major trans-Atlantic port. In the early days of the war, No. 37 MU (Maintenance Unit) was based at Burtonwood for the repair of aircraft damaged in the Battle of Britain. Provision for aircraft storage was also made here so that stocks of planes were ready for a major offensive.

Burtonwood serviced a wide variety of aircraft. Here planes were also modified immediately after manufacture to take radio and radar equipment, and of course weapons.

The airfield had a large number of hangars operated by civilian engineering and electrical firms such as Rootes and Salford Electrical Co. These companies recruited their workforce locally and from other parts of the country. Many local girls preferred to work there on plane assembly rather than work at the ordnance factory at

Risley Moss on the other side of the town. The women usually worked on electrical wiring, frame assembly, and put the 'Skin' over the aircraft frame. Conditions were strict but the pay was good. Normal working hours were from 8 am to 5.30 pm with an hour's lunch. Most evenings, workers had to keep going until 7 pm and they had only one day off at weekends. The journey from the centre of Warrington to Burtonwood could take up to an hour - especially in the blackout, so workers had very little free time. Security and discipline were very strictly enforced and one worker recalls being suspended for some days for clocking off a few minutes early. Workers had to carry identity cards with photographs at all times and never saw any other part of the base but their own. Holidays were limited and absence frowned on - even in the case of sickness. However the picture was not completely black. There were compensations - good pay and friendly atmosphere in each hangar. There were often social evenings and dances and of course the inevitable ENSA concerts!

Burtonwood's association with the Americans is well known. It was later in the war from 1942 onwards that Flying Fortresses, Liberators and GI's were filling every available square yard of the base. It seemed like another invasion to local people, by now well used to the sight of the unfamiliar faces of evacuees. Virtually overnight, a cultural revolution took place. The town and surrounding villages were flooded with comparatively wealthy servicemen, laden with chocolate, cigarettes and nylons - unfamiliar commodities to the ration-weary British!

Friction was inevitable. One Warrington dance hall was almost closed down because its manager allowed in a West Indian. This offended some Americans (used to a colour bar) and resulted in the hall becoming out of bounds to US and British service personnel. Townspeople were also worried about the possible effect all this would have on morals - particularly among local girls. It did nothing to allay their fears when they learned that the first batch of GIs to the town included a number of

*Aircraft "packed" at Burtonwood. (Flt. Sgt. R. Lackenback, courtesy of Warrington Guardian).*

criminals released from prison on condition that they enlisted!

For us it may be difficult to appreciate the impact of such an influx of servicemen on a relatively quiet area. The film "Yanks" (released around 1984) was actually based on Burtonwood and gives you a good idea if you have seen it. Apart from some initial friction, local people now recall how friendly, generous and homesick the GIs were and how they livened up the social life of the town considerably, jitterbugging in the dance halls and packing the cinemas nightly.

Sadly, fifty one years of British-American relations ended in 1993 when the base finally closed, and little now remains of it. It reached its peak in the late 1940s and early 1950s, when it played a major role in the postwar occupation of Europe by the Allies. Supply planes from Burtonwood took part in the Berlin Airlift. As you drive up Burtonwood Road, you can see government buildings on the right, part of the wartime base, and further up to the left of the roundabout, there are some hangars which now house industrial units. The bulk of the airfield has disappeared under the M62 and other development. However, when the base closed, the Burtonwood Association was formed to perpetuate the memory of all who worked and lived here and to establish a Heritage Centre. Anyone wanting to find out more can contact Yvonne Livesey of the Association on 01925 226606.

Let's return now via Hood Lane to the A57 and turn left towards the centre of the town. About one mile further on, just after the large roundabout, you will see the magnificent building of Joseph Crosfields Soap Works on the right. Soap may seem a strange essential of war. In fact it assumes great importance when you consider large groups of personnel herded together in camps - often in rough and ready conditions. Soap becomes vital to hygiene and disease control, so much of Crosfields' production during the war went to the Forces. This did not leave much for home consumption so Crosfields and Lever Bros had to place apologetic advertisements in local papers to comfort housewives who could not obtain the precious Puritan and Sunlight soaps! Incidentally, Crosfields also produced glycerine for use in explosives manufacture.

*Warrington Town Hall.*

Continue now into the centre of Warrington. It's advisable to park in one of the official car parks near the new shopping centre, GOLDEN SQUARE. In Sankey Street you will find on the left the TOWN HALL, which stands in Bank Park. Those magnificent gates were happily spared from the wartime salvage campaign.

Once you have parked, take a walk down Bold Street, passing the Club (which housed a public air raid shelter) on the left, Palmyra Square on the right, with its war memorial, and Parr Hall, where so many entertainments were held in wartime. A little further on the right stands WARRINGTON MUSEUM AND ART GALLERY, a marvellous Victorian building. Here you can see a few World War II exhibits and a display on the South Lancashire Regiment (the main exhibition is at Fulwood Barracks, Preston). It is interesting to remember that the Museum building housed an emergency information centre for the public during the War. Here local people would find leaflets on the blackout, air raid regulations and saving schemes. The local council organised many activities for the "Hometown Holidays for Warrington" scheme in co-operation with the RAF at Padgate and the US forces. The programme of events included a grand procession along Sankey Street with competitions for the Best Decorated Street, swimming galas, bowling contests, dances and concerts. This annual event seems to have done much to boost morale and also helped to relieve the pressure on the railways during the traditional holiday season (the original purpose of the scheme nationwide). Instead of seeking their pleasure elsewhere, people found it at home.

Let's continue down Bold Street to Wilson Patten Street (the A5061). From here you can see the site occupied by Thames Board Mills (behind the MFI store.) For a better view, walk along to the right and up Slutchers Lane. Located on the loop of the Mersey, Thames Board was a major local employer and produced many items, such as cardboard, vital to the war effort. Boxes for gas masks and emergency rations as well as packing for shells and Red Cross parcels were made here.

Thames Board Mills was a typical example of a well organised factory. It had its own firewatchers, Civil Defence squad and Home Guard and Auxilliary Fire Service. Employees took part in blood transfusion schemes and National Savings Schemes and there was also a fund set up to send money and gifts to workers who were serving in the Forces.

The employees even had their own sports ground adjacent to the factory. Here many social events were held for the workers and their families and friends. But one fine Saturday afternoon in 1940 disaster struck when a stray German plane flying over Warrington unloaded its cargo

*Above: Home Guard, Thames Board Mills, Warrington.*

*Below: Fire and Civil Defence Squad, Thames Board Mills, Warrington. (Imperial War Museum).*

*Aftermath of the raid on Thames Board's sports ground.*

of bombs on to the recreation field while a fete was in progress. The result was 16 people killed, 15 severely injured and 28 more slightly wounded - a sad end to a happy afternoon. The factory and sports club escaped with only minor damage but the memory of that fateful day lingered long in local people's minds especially when they remembered that a number of children had been among the casualties.

Thames Board and Crosfields were not the only factories in Warrington aiding the war effort. There were many others making enormous contributions such as Rylands, and Lockers' wire works, whose products ranged from wire mesh for gas masks to springs for gun mechanisms and tank suspensions. Other locally made items included prefabricated ships and landing craft, Morrison shelters, shell casings, Mulberry Harbour sections, and chemicals such as toluene and naphthalene.

When you consider the variety of industry and military bases in and around Warrington, the town was fortunate to escape serious bombing. Luftwaffe maps and aerial photographs show the German High Command was well aware of the key installations around the town. Apart from the gas and electricity works, there were large grain storage facilities on the river. Their destruction would have been a severe blow to food supplies. A direct hit on one of the bridges or on the Ship Canal would have disrupted communications. The Canal was after all busy with boats, carrying food, which had braved the hazards of the Atlantic convoys. Local people can remember crewmen throwing bananas - a precious commodity - to children on the shore. We know that the local barracks and Risley Moss Ordnance factory were also on the German target list.

There were nights when local people rushed to the air raid shelters in each street, clutching their insurance policies and other valuables, but as time passed many preferred to take their chances in their own homes and reinforced the space under the stairs. One man did so after seeing how staircases remained intact despite severe bomb damage at New Brighton, just down the river.

Warrington was really saved from heavy bombing by Germany's need to concentrate on Liverpool and Manchester. But local weather conditions in this section of the Mersey Valley played an important part in the town's defence. Swirling mists and fog often screened Warrington from air attack and thanks to this there has been no need for massive re-development of the town centre. Although there has, of course, been some rebuilding and modernisation, many of the buildings, like the names of the streets, survive to retain the town's essential character.

*Bomb damage in Warrington.*

Leaving the centre of Warrington now on the A57 Leigh/ Manchester Road, turn left opposite the cemetery into Padgate Lane. Take the first left into Marsh House Lane and third right into O'Leary Street, and on the right you will see Peninsula Barracks, now mainly used by the Territorial Army. Let's return now to Marsh House Lane and go straight ahead at the traffic lights into Padgate Lane, turning left at the roundabout on to the A50 (Orford Road). A quarter of a mile further on, turn right on to the A574 Birchwood Way for this road cuts through the former RAF camp at Padgate where raw recruits began their basic training - especially in the days of National Service. Now the only reminder that the camp was there is in the streetnames of a nearby housing estate. Look for "Andover", "Anson", "Blenheim", "Biggin" etc, and remember as you pass by the playing fields that all this once formed part of the extensive camp grounds.

Continue now on the A574 for another two miles until you cross the M6. Turn right at the next roundabout for Oakwood Gate. Here turn left into Ordnance Avenue and continue on for almost half a mile until you see RISLEY MOSS NATURE PARK on the right hand side, with Birchwood Forest Park on the left.

This area was the site of a huge ordnance factory complex which covered more than two square miles. Originally a peat bog, Risley became the site of one of the new munitions works urgently needed when rearmament began after the Munich crisis of 1938. By September 1940, production was in full swing. But because of tight security, relatively little is known about what went on inside Risley's well guarded fences.

Even today it is hard to find detailed information. We do know that Risley was a filling factory where shell castings and explosive materials (made in separate, small engineering plants and chemical works all over the country) were brought together for the final stages of assembly and shipment. The work, therefore, was highly dangerous. Safety was a prime consideration and in order to contain the risk of explosion and fire within a specific area, the site was divided into sections by a grid road system with well spaced

*Risley Moss Royal Ordnance Factory.*

assembly sheds. Batches of shells were filled in limited numbers so that there was never a stockpile of potentially explosive material lying around.

Special clothing was issued to all workers, including overalls and shoes. Metal fastenings, jewellery and even hairpins were banned to reduce the risk of sparks. Like Burtonwood, workers were restricted to their own sections of the site and had no knowledge of work being done outside their own unit. Consequently we know little about any accidents that occurred here. Injuries to hands seem to have been common - although workers were supposed to wear gloves - and a moment's carelessness often resulted in accidents with fingers severely damaged or lost.

Fatal accidents did occur but again information is scarce. There are stories of sheds mysteriously blowing up and workers at Risley must have suffered badly from stress brought on by the constant risk and need for caution. Many of them - notably women working with toxic chemicals - suffered from skin disorders, lost their hair and also suffered from liver and kidney problems. (This is reminiscent of the First World War when ordnance workers were nicknamed "Canaries" because the chemicals turned their skin yellow.)

*Risley Moss today.*

Today, much of the ordnance factory site has been taken over by housing development and by Risley Moss Nature Park. There are some pleasant walks along wooded paths and views over the mossland - a far cry from the wartime scene when the area was lined with assembly sheds and crossed by railway tracks and trucks loaded with shells and ammunition. Risley Moss Visitor Centre has a display on the ecology and history of the Moss and is open daily except Friday. Telephone 01925 824339 for more information.

Our next port of call is the village of HIGH LEGH which lies four or five miles south of Warrington on the A50 (accessible from the town centre or Junction 20 off the M6). To the left of the A50, opposite a garden centre, private houses now stand on part of the former army camp. Here chilly huts provided uncomfortable accommodation for soldiers and ATS recruits undergoing initial training. The land is privately owned and therefore not accessible but it is worth noting before turning off the A50 to the right and making for ARLEY HALL, where our journey takes us next.

Arley Hall was made available to the Red Cross and St John Ambulance Brigade at the outbreak of war. Here in this lovely Victorian building they ran a jointly organised and staffed Residential Nursery for young evacuees from London. Some three years or so later, the Hall became a Red Cross Convalescent Home for patients from Winwick Hospital near Warrington which specialised in orthopaedic cases. Part of the Hall, including the Library, continued to be privately occupied and the estate's life went on as normal. Part of the land was requisitioned as an airfield - Appleton Thorn became part of Liverpool's defences and was later taken over by the Fleet Air Arm.

As in other parts of the country, there was a division of the LDV (Home Guard) stationed here which included staff from the Arley Estate. Enemy bombers did pass overhead regularly en route to Liverpool and bombs were dropped here but fortunately damage was slight. The Park was sometimes used as a training area for troops on exercises - the men would be billeted in the stables while their officers bedded down more comfortably in the library.

Arley Hall and Gardens are open to the public afternoons from April to October. Closed Mondays except on Bank Holidays. For more details, telephone Arley 01565 777353.

---

**OTHER PLACES TO VISIT**

▶ *Stockley Farm, Arley.*
*Tel: 01565 777323*

---

62

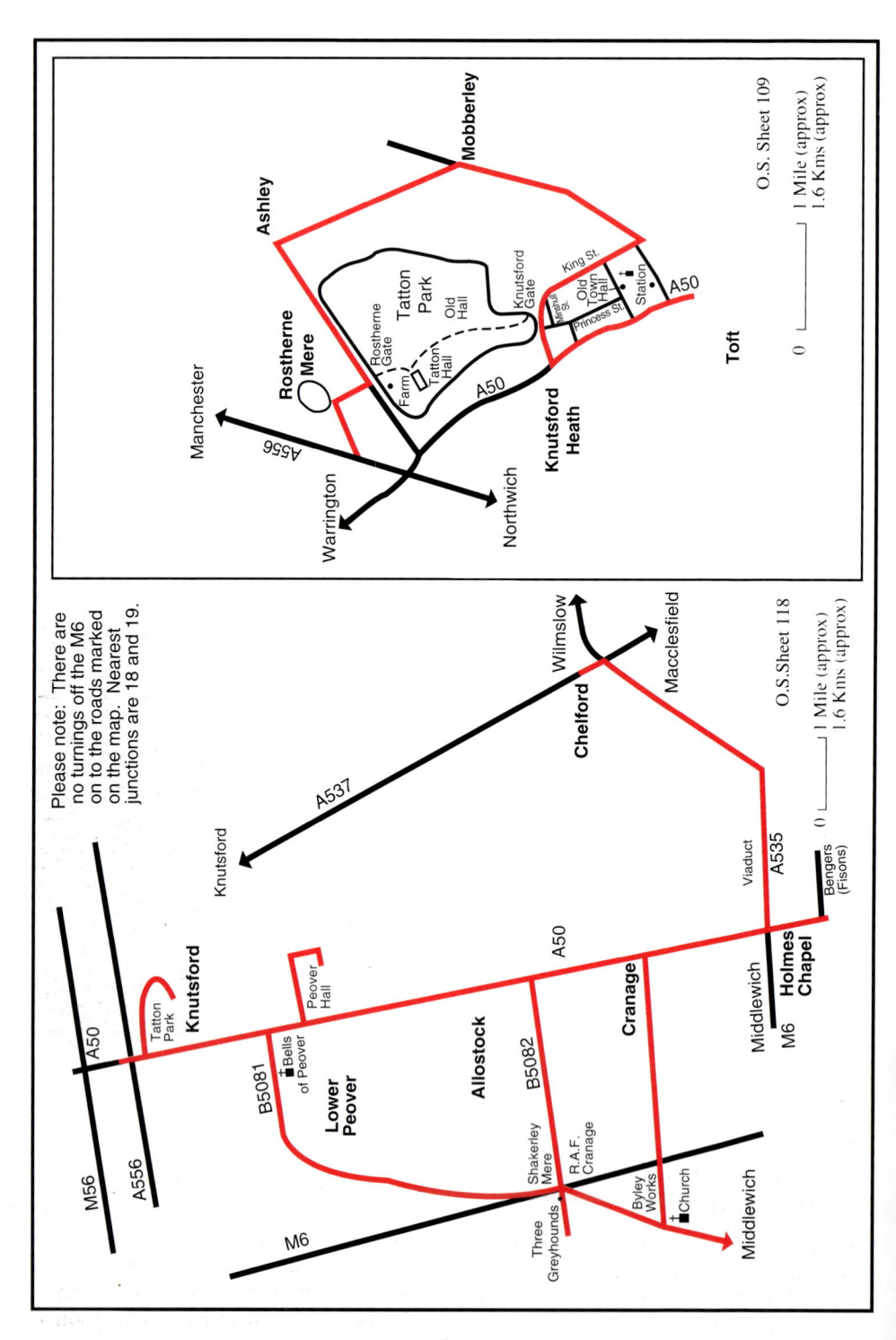

# The Knutsford area in Wartime

## *Men Dropping from the Skies*

Perhaps Knutsford is best known for its gracious architecture, attractive shops, and the nearby stately home, TATTON PARK, home of the Egerton family for generations. Some may recall that the town lay on the traditional coaching road to London and others that it was for a time home of the famous Victorian writer, Mrs Gaskell, who based her novel "Cranford" on the town. Most people would be surprised to learn of the significant role Knutsford played during the war, but the town's position rendered it safe from German bombing and so it became a refuge for evacuees and a major billeting area for the Forces. Even Tatton Park itself was to be involved in the war effort and here, in the now peaceful parkland, some of the most exciting and intensive military training of the War took place. Thus the people of Knutsford quite rightly felt they were playing an important part in the war effort.

A little to the north of Knutsford lie the mansion and parkland of TATTON. You can find them easily by following signs from the A50 and the A556. The house and estate were owned by Maurice, Lord Egerton and immediately war was declared he was anxious to put them to good use in the national interest. In his younger days he had been a keen flyer so he particularly wanted the RAF to have first claim on the park for training.

*Tatton Park*

As the war progressed, the RAF was to use a large part of the Park as the Dropping Zone (DZ) for parachutists training at Ringway (today's Manchester International Airport). His lordship was to take much interest in this training but his loyalty to the RAF did not prevent him from becoming exasperated from time to time with the discourtesy of some of the pilots and trainees. One such incident occurred when a converted Whitley Bomber (used to drop trainee parachutists) crashed into his rhododendron bushes in May 1943 and the offending pilot made no attempt to apologise! This area was subsequently christened "The Whitley Gap". To be fair, Lord Egerton was mainly concerned about the safety of the Whitleys, since the failure of one engine could mean that the aircraft would crash - he was by no means only anxious about his garden.

To use the Park as Ringway's DZ meant a certain amount of upheaval. Many trees were felled, huts erected near the Rostherne Drive to accommodate the RAF ground personnel, and a balloon site and roadways were also constructed. Security of course was of the utmost importance in those days - a consideration which affected the running of the whole estate. Even his lordship had to show his pass at the gate.

*Barrage balloons in Tatton Park.*

Barrage balloons were used over Tatton Park during the time and one - known as "Bessie" - was equipped with a cage suspended underneath from which trainee parachutists made their intermediate jumps after basic training in the hangar at Ringway. The jump from the cage was thought by many to be even more terrifying than a jump out of a moving aircraft at high altitude. This was the final stage in training which also took place over Tatton Park. The cage was a necessary evil and occasionally even a source of amusement when the retaining cable from the ground snapped and "Bessie" made her escape, sometimes with the parachute instructor trapped inside! His precipitate exit must have seemed like sweet revenge to his pupils on the ground below! Once, the escaping "Bessie" caused havoc to telegraph wires and electricity cables as she cavorted southwards across the country before being brought down more than halfway to London!

*The "cage".*

Trainees well remember the relief of safe arrival on the ground and the reward of a strong cup of tea from a small canteen in the Park before they returned by bus to Ringway.

Tatton was also the scene of more watery exploits. ROSTHERNE MERE (now a national nature reserve) became the target for parachute drops into water. Such a jump became the Christmas ritual for Wing Commander Maurice Newnham, the Commanding Officer of No. 1 PTS at Ringway.

*Wing Commander Newnham.*

Troops also practiced night drops into Rostherne. So did the SOE agents (Special Operations Executive) who underwent parachute training at Ringway from the earliest days of the war. They were always listed as Mr X or Miss Y on the flight manifest. One Dutch agent caused great alarm one night when the boat waiting to pick him up after his jump into Rostherne was unable to find any trace of him - in spite of a major search. When the backup team gave up hope of finding him and eventually returned to base, utterly depressed, they were met by the sight of the Dutchman warming himself by the fire and drinking brandy! He then disarmed them completely by explaining that he had decided that if he could elude his friends, who knew exactly where to look for him, he would stand a good chance of avoiding capture when he was ultimately dropped in the Zuider Zee!

Inevitably, there were tragic accidents. One man was killed early in the training programme and a new parachute design was adopted to reduce the risk. However, all paratroops dreaded the possibility of "candling" which happened when the

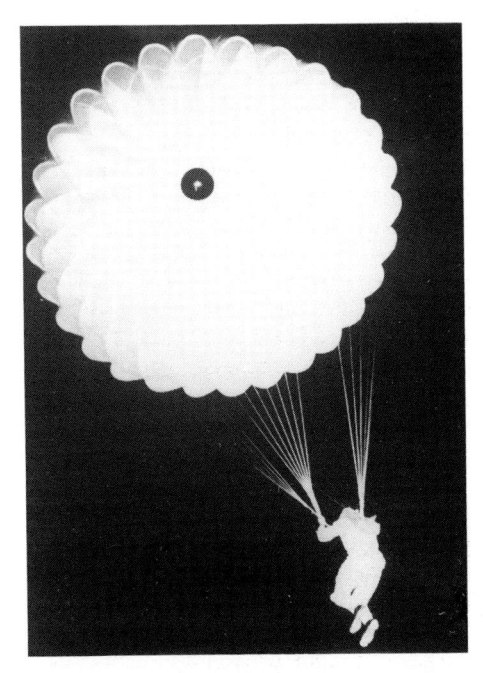

*Parachuting at night. (Imperial War Museum).*

parachute strings twisted together and the parachute failed to open. After such an accident, the parachute instructors made "confidence jumps" from the cage or aircraft to restore their trainees' morale. It was distressing for all concerned when such a tragedy happened, but taken as a whole, the accident record was good when you consider that 60,000 men were trained in the course of the war.

Minor accidents were common - like sprains and twisted ankles. There were even some fractures such as that suffered by the author Evelyn Waugh, perhaps best known for the novel "Brideshead Revisited". Several well-known personalities, such as Richard Todd, the actor and Frank Muir of radio and TV fame, were among the thousands who jumped over Tatton Park.

Lord Egerton regarded the RAF with respect - apart from a few minor incidents - but the same could not be said of his attitude towards the Army. They also occupied part of the Park (mainly the Little Park, near the HOME FARM) where there was a tented encampment for the succession of regiments based there. The Army also took over part of the stable block and even stored ammunition at the OLD HALL (home of earlier owners of Tatton) much to Lord Egerton's alarm and indignation. He was horrified at their lack of responsibility towards his property so his relations with successive camp commanders were strained. He expected his permission to be sought before the grounds were dug up and was furious at the Army's lack of consideration for the agricultural side of the estate. Troops disturbed stock, destroyed crops and broke branches off trees. He was often disturbed by the laxity and indiscipline he saw in some officers, particularly those who did not use the entrance to the Park allocated to the Army and ordered their men to scale the wall as a short cut.

Lord Egerton's exasperation is understandable, though he must have been considered a nuisance by Western Command. He kept up a continuous stream of complaints by letter, demanding immediate redress. He also tried to pull strings in London and even contemplated a direct appeal to the King but apparently thought better of it - his letter was never sent. Yet there was another side to his character, for among the heaps of correspondence complaining about the Army's abuse of his hospitality are notes expressing concern about the welfare of the ordinary soldier. It could have been "noblesse oblige", but he issued an invitation for sick men using the stable yard for recreation to go into the garden on fine days. A local man who had suffered a nervous breakdown in India has reason to be grateful to Lord Egerton too for he tried to gain the man's discharge and early return home. Can this be the same man who complained about the Army's behaviour at High Legh: "My neighbour, My Cornewall Legh of High Legh has had his cellar broken into by the soldiery quartered there, and his 100 bottles of port have afforded them a delightfully drunken orgy... This is really not good enough."

Again the human side of Lord Egerton's character can be seen in his concern for men hospitalised in Knutsford. He often visited them in the Bexton Road Hospital and brought patients who were fit enough for a day out at Tatton. There he would drive them around the grounds and give them tea. Often he entertained young evacuees, taking them boating on the lake, and was amused by their artless comments on the servants, and revelations about their own way of life. One 8 year old from Manchester told him he had been taught to beg on Piccadilly, or steal, if he wanted to avoid a thrashing from his father!

*Bexton Road Hospital, Knutsford.*

Lord Egerton and his Agent were also occupied with the routine running of the estate. Like so many other landowners his lordship was under pressure from the War Ag to cultivate additional acres and he was often in dispute with the local committee when they selected land which was unsuitable or too expensive to cultivate. There was also the inevitable problem of manpower to cope with. The estate's own fire service suffered particularly from this as the war progressed.

Lord Egerton was thus in the unenviable position of trying to keep control of his estate and doing all he could for the war effort. Most landowners simply left their estates for the duration, but Lord Egerton wanted to stay in his family home and to feel he was helping the war effort in some way. Frequently, when the interests of the Air Force, Army and War Ag conflicted, he felt himself ignored as wartime bureaucracy took over. He tried to carry on "as normal", preserving the fiction that officers billeted in his home were his guests. He did make them welcome, though, for they were allowed full use of the house, though arrangements were made for their meals to be prepared in the Butler's pantry. In return, he expected his guests to look after his furniture and books in the library and was very annoyed at any damage. He liked to know who had arrived or departed and to receive a polite note of thanks from guests - an old fashioned courtesy, perhaps, but remember that Maurice Egerton was well into his sixties when war broke out.

He even allowed some of his guests and officers billeted in the Knutsford area to shoot duck in the Park, and was generous with gifts of game and venison to the Officers' Mess at Ringway.

*Lord Egerton with an American guest*

The war must have proved extremely trying for Lord Egerton as he attempted to control the various factions laying claim to the Park. Naturally he was concerned that the treasures of his house should not be put at risk from bomb damage if Tatton became a target, a possibility which was increased by the Army's presence, the Dropping Zone and the later storage of aircraft and tanks under the trees prior to D-Day.

He relaxed a little, however, by organising the planting of the fine rhododendrons in the garden with the help of the Land Girls from the estate.

Tatton Park is open to the public: the house has seen little change since the Second World War - the display in the Tenants' Hall includes Lord Egerton's wartime trophy, a bomb (now defused) which landed in the Park. There is a wartime trail leading visitors round the main sites of interest and you can see the Home Farm at Tatton Dale almost exactly as it was in the war years. The Park, which is open to visitors all year round, contains a MEMORIAL TO THE AIRBORNE FORCES, many of whom still return to visit the Dropping Zone where they trained. For opening times ring 01565 750250.

We go now to visit the villages to the east of Tatton Park - Rostherne, Ashley and Mobberley. These were often used as mock

*The Tatton Park bomb.*

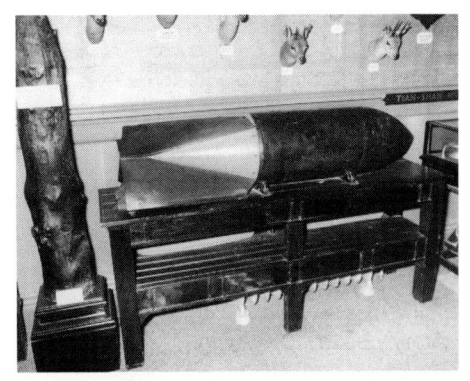

battle grounds by paratroops on exercise who would land in Tatton Park and then fight their way into "enemy territory" - only to be met at Ashley or Mobberley Stations by the ladies of the WI proffering tea and sandwiches! ROSTHERNE, once part of the Tatton Estate, is still quite untouched by new development. It certainly saw its share of servicemen during the war years - one local lady remembers the church collection being taken in a GI helmet one Sunday!

You can drive from Tatton Park to Knutsford via Rostherne, Ashley and Mobberley by following the signs on the country roads - a pleasant detour. Or you can go directly into the town via the the park's Knutsford Gate by turning right up Garden Road to reach the main A50 Manchester Road. You will see Knutsford Heath directly ahead. This area, a favourite place for walkers, was used as an Army encampment during the war. Turning left now, head for the town centre and take a walk around Knutsford itself. A stroll around the town is always pleasant for it is rightly famed for its attractive and varied architecture. Look out for the surprisingly Italian flavour of Richard Harding Watt's designs.

When war was declared, evacuee trains poured into this small country town. The situation called for good organisation on the part of the local billeting officer and the WVS. They and other voluntary organisations met evacuees at the station, and the local newspaper reported that "the hostesses carried the suitcases" for their visitors. There was some resistance from a few households, but the majority rallied round to meet the emergency.

The WVS again was heavily involved in the continued welfare of the child evacuees. It set up a hospital at Rockford Lodge, and organised clothing exchanges for the needy ones. Local ladies were also active in knitting troops' comforts.

In the lower part of the town, halfway along King Street from the station, stands the ROYAL GEORGE HOTEL. Here lunches were served to evacuee children with the assistance of the WVS. This helped to relieve the pressure on families accommodating the children. The George later became a favourite haunt of American soldiers and many have since returned to visit their old "watering hole". Even General Patton frequently called in for a drink here when he was based at Peover Hall.

Another long established inn, THE ANGEL HOTEL, can be found along King Street. Here, the WVS organised a rest centre for older people evacuated into the area, and it became a meeting place for adults evacuated to the town.

To reach the other main shopping thoroughfare, walk up Minshull Street and turn left along Princess Street. Where this street meets the main road, you will find the former KNUTSFORD TOWN HALL, a brick built building in the Gothic style, now

*King Street, Knutsford.*

68

a furniture store, and Post Office. During wartime it was used by various local organisations but it is famous because here on 25th April 1944, General Patton made the speech which caused his downfall.

*The Old Town Hall, Knutsford.*

Patton, already a controversial figure, had been invited to make a speech at a ceremony to open a Donut Dugout for American troops in the area. Organised by the WVS, the occasion was intended to be informal, without major Press coverage. However, Patton was "news" so a number of reporters attended. Patton's speech was lively and patriotic. He expressed the opinion that the world was destined to be ruled by the American, British and Russian peoples - but the version that reached America omitted to mention the Soviet Union. Patton was immediately condemned for slighting a vital ally - a serious political gaffe, inexcusable for such a high-ranking officer. He already had a reputation for thoughtless and aggressive behaviour, and his ambition had won him many enemies. They lost no time in using this incident to discredit him, and so Patton lost any chance of gaining a major command position in the forthcoming campaign in Europe.

Let's leave Knutsford now and drive south on the A50. On the right you will see TOFT HALL which is set back from the road. On the opposite side, look out for TOFT CHURCH. Land here was used as the site of a POW camp for various nationalities until 1948.

About half a mile outside Knutsford, turn right for Lower Peover (pronounced "Peever") and follow signs for the "BELLS OF PEOVER" which you will find up a lane to the left, next to St Oswald's Church.

This inn dates from around the 13th century and is noted for its connection with General Patton, a regular visitor when he was based nearby. Locals well remember his geniality and both he and his staff enjoyed the opportunity to relax here. Eisenhower even joined Patton on one occasion for lunch.

The then-landlady had connections with the theatre and actors and actresses playing in Manchester often used to stay here at that time. Jack Buchanan, Vivien Leigh, Noel Coward and Laurence Olivier are all believed to have "slept" here!

Set in charming surroundings, the "Bells of Peover" provides lunches and evening meals. Unfortunately it no longer offers residential accommodation.

Let's return now to the A50 and turn right for half a mile. Next turn left at the "Whipping Stocks" for Over-Peover. Half a mile from here, you will find a footpath

*Lower Peover.*

leading to St Laurence's Church and Peover Hall, next to the church. You can drive round to PEOVER HALL if you prefer, just following the signs, but casual visitors are discouraged. The Hall was requisitioned from the Mainwaring family and was used by Patton as a HQ during preparations for the Normandy Landings. The house has changed a good deal since the last war, and the 18th century wing which Patton occupied has been demolished. The Tudor portion which remains has been extensively restored. This section was little used by Patton's staff but the Drawing Room did serve as the Officers' Mess. Two or three hundred American troops lived in huts in the park and from 1945-50 the Hall and grounds were used as a Civilian Resettlement Unit which enabled former prisoners of war to readjust to civilian life. This process of adaptation was not easy for men who had been in captivity for some years. Here they had the opportunity to rediscover old skills, enjoy sport and recreation and so become acclimatised to life in post-war Britain.

Peover Hall is only open on Monday (except Bank Holidays) and Thursday afternoons from May to end September. Telephone 01565 722656 for further information.

Patton was a regular worshipper at St Laurence's close to the Hall and the flag (nicknamed "Old Glory") he presented to the church still hangs there. Polish prisoners (probably German sympathisers) from Toft Camp mentioned previously, built part of the church wall and you should look for their names carved in the stone.

Next, we make for SHAKERLEY MERE, about five miles down the A50. Turn right on to the B5082 and just after crossing the M6 you will see the Mere on your right. It's a popular spot with walkers and picnickers and there is parking available.

*General G.S. Patton. (Courtesy of U.S. Dept of Defense).*

To continue our journey, drive up to the crossroads where the B5082 intersects with the B5081 Middlewich Road. On these crossroads stands the "THREE GREYHOUNDS", a very popular pub frequented by airmen and ground crew from the RAF base at Cranage and Byley airfield works, located on the left of the B5081 towards Middlewich. This site was requisitioned in haste and several farmers were forced to leave their homes and land.

The airfield ground was soft so the runways were reinforced with interlocking steel mesh. Many huts were provided as accommodation for airmen as well as hangars for the necessary maintenance section (who also put together Wellington Bombers here). There was also a gym where dances were held and existing buildings such as farmhouses were pressed into service (where they were not demolished to make way for the landing strip and dispersal areas). The white bungalow you can see opposite Shakerley Mere - just north of the pub - was used as a base hospital.

The airmen were generally popular with the locals, for the night fighters who flew out of Cranage to defend the North West deserved respect. But one "townie" will never forget the lecture he received for walking through a field of growing wheat, which he had thought was grass!

Let's drive now down the B5081 to BYLEY and turn left at the church. Here, the churchyard contains the graves of a German bomber crew who crashed nearby. Travelling along this road you pass the maintenance and construction area of the airfield. You cannot readily explore the field for the land has now been returned to farming. Today little remains of the buildings, which were either demolished or sold off when the airfield finally ceased to function after a period as an American base after the war.

Byley Lane rejoins the A50 at Cranage. Let's turn right here for one and a half miles until you reach the centre of HOLMES CHAPEL. This was a quiet village until the advent of the M6 made it a convenient place for commuters to live. Holmes Chapel was an obvious place to send evacuee children in 1939 - so many that the local school had to work shifts! Although some evacuees' ways seemed strange to the local people, the children soon settled down. Nevertheless, few hostesses will never forget the horror of discovering that their little charges were infested with head lice!

Holmes Chapel had little industry in those days. Bengers, the invalid food manufacturers, had moved here in 1938 and were producing vital food supplements on the site now owned by Fisons, on the A50. The Crown Wallpaper Works (now Fine Art Wall Coverings Ltd.) on the A535 Macclesfield Road packed shells as part of its war production. The villagers were of course involved in the usual fund-raising events to help the war effort - whist drives and dances were held in the Victoria Club. In rural areas such as this the WI was active in gathering herbs and plants for medicinal use. There was a national campaign at that time to collect rose hips in Autumn for the manufacture of syrup - its Vitamin C content was vital now that supplies of citrus fruits like oranges were very scarce.

About one mile outside Holmes Chapel on the A535, look for a long row of arches forming the railway viaduct on the Crewe-Manchester line on the left. This was one of the key defence points for the local Home Guard who patrolled it nightly in case of saboteurs - a far from pleasant duty, made all the more difficult by the narrow space between the track and the parapet, which meant the guard on duty was in some danger when a train passed through. Let's continue on this road for 5 miles to CHELFORD. Chelford's large agricultural market is well-known and during the last war large quantities of food were stored here in a Government warehouse close to the railway sidings. The building (now Irlam Storage) can still be seen adjacent to the "Dixon Arms" which lies on the left hand side of the road to Knutsford.

### OTHER PLACES TO VISIT

▶ **Knutsford Heritage Centre.** Tel: 01565 650506

▶ **Jodrell Bank Science Centre and Arboretum, near Holmes Chapel** Tel: 01477 571339

▶ **Tabley House, Knutsford** (unusual wartime memorabilia of the Leicester family) Tel: 01565 750151

▶ **The Tabley Old School Cuckoo Clock Museum** Tel: 01565 633039

▶ **Hillside Ornamental Fowl, Mobberley** Tel: 01565 873282

72

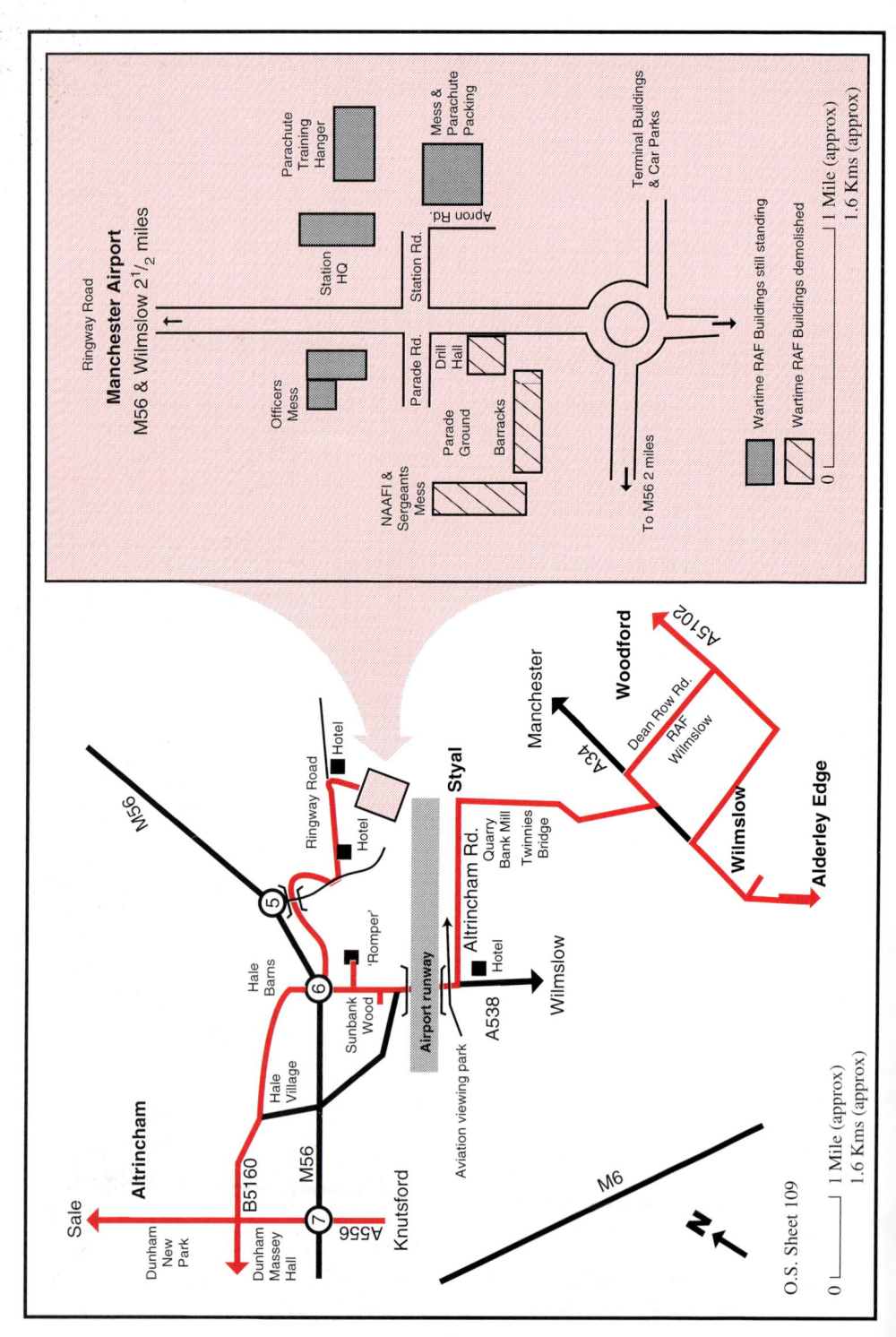

# Ringway and the Airborne Forces

## *The Great Innovation of World War II*

*At the time of going to print there are major road building projects both planned and under way in the Wilmslow - Handforth areas. This inevitably means that some of the directions in this chapter will change. We apologise for any inconvenience this may cause.*

Ringway, Manchester's airport, played a unique role in modern warfare in Britain. It was here that the novel military technique of dropping men by parachute into the battle zone was developed and perfected. During those wartime years, parachute training was to become the principal activity at Ringway, overshadowing and displacing other experimental developments also originating there.

Thus the security and defence of the airfield, together with the billeting and training facilities associated with this innovation soon expanded beyond the official boundaries of the RAF station and small municipal airport which Ringway had been in 1939. Life within a ten mile radius of the airport inevitably became affected by this new activity, particularly when we recall that the area also played a major part in the country's aircraft industry, with production hangars at Ringway itself as well as the Fairey and A.V. Roe factories at Heaton Chapel,

Chadderton, and Woodford, and the Metropolitan Vickers works at Trafford Park.

It would be impossible to cover the whole area affected by the RAF's activities at Ringway, but the section which stretches from Altrincham to just beyond Wilmslow holds many interesting connections with

*Parachute training.*

the airfield and has many other wartime associations worthy of note. It is here then that our journey begins.

Let's start our tour at the major roundabout on the A556/ A56/ M56 by taking the A56 towards Altrincham. When you reach the first set of traffic lights, turn left for DUNHAM MASSEY HALL. Almost at once you will see on the left a group of large houses, partly hidden by bushes. One of these, Dunham Lodge, is now converted into flats, but during wartime it was here that the secret agents of SOE (Special Operations Executive) stayed while undergoing parachute training at Ringway. For security reasons, they had to be kept

*Violette Szarbo*

separate from the rest of the trainees and of course their real names were never used on training records. Odette Churchill and Violette Szabo, both eventually captured and tortured by the Gestapo, trained at Ringway. (Violette Szabo was later executed at Ravensbruck.)

Dunham Massey itself had been a military hospital in the Great War but in the Second World War it remained a private residence. The Countess of Stamford, who was a local patron of the Red Cross, did however take an active interest in the war effort, as did Lord Stamford, and many foreign delegations were entertained at the house. The visitors' book bears witness to this and in it we can find the signatures of Soviet visitors as well as that of Princess Mary, and Princess Royal, who visited the county quite often on inspection tours of Red Cross work and the women's services such as FANY and the ATS.

Like so many other large estates, Dunham suffered from the inevitable shortage of manpower that war brings. Luckily, it sustained no serious physical damage although it was within the range of marauding German bombers attacking Manchester. Its only victim was one of the Lodges and there is a photograph of this on display in the Chintz Drawing Room.

If you would like to visit Dunham Massey Hall, it is open every afternoon, April to October. Telephone 0161 941 1025 for further details.

To continue our tour return now to the A56 and turn left. Soon you will see on the left part of the DUNHAM FOREST GOLF CLUB, set in Dunham New Park. In wartime, and for a period afterwards, this was the site of a prisoner of war camp (the entrance to the camp can still be identified by the curve in the kerbstones across the footpath). It was here that prisoners were interrogated for information by skilled linguists, before the process of de-Nazification began, enabling them to be declared fit for repatriation. Any prisoners considered reliable enough were sent out to work on nearby farms. Sometimes, though, their presence and apparent freedom was bitterly criticised by local people with memories of the Manchester blitz or of friends and relatives killed in action still fresh in their minds. In their spare time, prisoners often turned to craft work, using

On reaching Dunham lights, take the left turn for Hale. Follow the B5357 which leads through Hale Village shopping centre, known as Ashley Road, until on the outskirts of the village you find Madely Close on the left hand side. Opposite it, behind the railings of a private garden, see if you can spot a curious circular concrete block with a steel pin in the centre. This is the mount for a spigot mortar. Several of these must have been dotted around the area as part of the ground defences of Ringway.

Continue now down Ashley Road and fork left into Castle Mill Lane. At Castle Mill Bridge there is a footpath which leads off to the left towards Sunbank Wood. Here, overlooking the bridge, below a small bluff in the woods, you can find another spigot mortar mount.

Sunbank Wood stretches north of Sunbank Lane - a walk of perhaps half a mile. As an alternative, you can continue on Castle Mill Lane to the A538 Wilmslow/ Altrincham Road and turn left into Sunbank Lane. There is parking here and you can spend some time observing the bird life for which the wood is well-known. Standing on Sunbank Lane is a

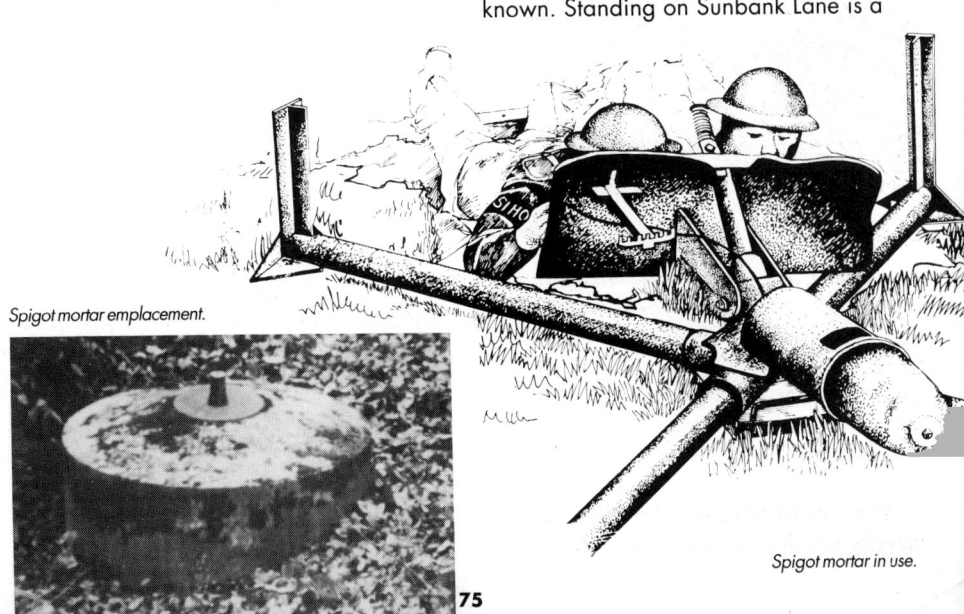

*The "Bavarian Castle" made by P.O.W.s at Dunham.*

waste materials - many people recall a "castle" entirely built from scrap, which once stood near the gates to the Park.

Almost opposite Dunham POW Camp, on the left stands DENZELL HOUSE, where evacuees were housed during the war. Today it houses offices.

*Spigot mortar emplacement.*

*Spigot mortar in use.*

75

large private house called "Hale Bank". Here WAAFs stationed at Ringway were housed. One WAAF lucky enough to have been billeted there recalls the unbelievable luxury of a private bathroom, comfortable sitting rooms - and even the use of a tennis court! Eventually only WAAFs detailed as parachute packers were housed there as the peaceful surroundings made it ideal for shift workers.

Head for the A538 now and make for Hale Barns and MANCHESTER AIRPORT. The Airport, with 13 million passengers a year, is one of the busiest in the country and among the top twenty in the world. It has expanded rapidly in the last few years with the building of a vast new Terminal 2 and new feeder roads. However, a small nucleus of World War II buildings still exists near Terminal 1. If you wish to track down the remains, we suggest you take the following route (not the shortest, but the easiest to describe).

After passing under the M56 turn left at the traffic lights into Runger Lane. Continue for 1 1/2 miles to the Hilton Hotel roundabout. Take the first left here into Ringway Road West and after 1/2 mile turn 1st right and you will soon see the Airport Hotel on your left. Just before you arrive at the roundabout by Terminal One you will see Parade Road a cul de sac, on the right. (We suggest you park in one of the short term car parks if you wish to view the area). The plan on page 72 will help you orient yourself.

Parade Road led into the RAF Parade ground (now a car park) and was enclosed on three sides by buildings. On the left, was the Drill Hall - known as St Christopher's - once used as a gymnasium, for pay parades and church services, and by the YMCA as a social club. The building in the centre was originally a block of barracks. Lack of accommodation was a permanent problem at Ringway

which often resulted in as many as 1500 people being billeted outside the camp (records show this number occupying a council estate in Wythenshawe). On the right of the square stood the Sergeants' Mess and NAAFI.

The Officers' Mess was situated on Ringway Road and opposite it on Station Road were the main HQ buildings where communications and administration staff worked. Behind this, you will find the hangar used for parachute training and opposite on the corner of Apron Road is the building where WAAFs packed the parachutes, under a large sign issuing the stern warning that "A Man's Life Depends On Every Parachute You Pack". Incidentally, in Terminal 1's Prayer Room there is a large glass mosaic window panel memorial to the thousands of parachutists who trained at Ringway.

At the outbreak of war Ringway had not long been operational as a commercial civilian airfield, under the control of Manchester City Corporation.

However, it was already the home of No. 613 (City of Manchester) squadron of the Auxilliary Air Force, but with the beginning of hostilities, this squadron left for active service and was based elsewhere.

As Ringway was not in the front line, it was ideally placed for training and experimental work. It was imperative that the RAF should match, and surpass, the enemy's techniques of aerial warfare, for the Spanish Civil War had shown the world that air supremacy was of vital importance to victory.

Churchill's arrival at No.10 Downing Street hastened activity in this direction. A Central Landing School was set up at Ringway and parachute training began. Pupils learned the basic techniques of

*Polish paratroopers at Ringway.*

landing - often easier than actually getting out of the aircraft - in the hangar at Ringway mentioned previously. Converted Whitley bombers with a hole cut out of the floor were to be used for the actual jumps so a simulated exit was erected in the training hangar. The exit "hole" proved rather a tight fit in the cumbersome gear of the parachutist and the unlucky ones were liable to catch their chins on the edge. This experience was ironically christened "The Whitley Kiss" *(see page ii)*. Later on Dakotas were used for parachuting and they proved less painful!

The second stage of training was known as "The Cage". Here the parachutist was hoisted in a cage suspended under a large barrage balloon at Tatton Park, designated as the Dropping Zone (DZ) for No. 1 PTS (Parachute Training School). The trainees usually hated this part of their training because the silent swaying of the cage as it was winched up was pretty nerve-racking.

Once these stages were complete only one thing remained - the live jump from a moving aeroplane over Tatton Park. The parachute was opened by a static line so all the parachutist had to worry about - apart from the risk of "Candling" - was finding a safe spot to land. (Not always an easy task, when you consider the number of trees in the Park.)

Success in this final stage of training meant that there could now be no turning back for the trainees, who became fully fledged members of the Airborne Forces. From now on, a refusal to jump resulted in court martial. Before, trainees were still volunteers and were at liberty to decide that parachuting was too much for them - although it took considerable courage to admit that the fear could not be controlled.

Ringway was also the scene of much wartime romance. This was hardly surprising when you consider the number of men undergoing training there. The

A Ringway wedding.

WAAFs on the station found themselves very much in demand - especially if they worked as parachute packers - and there were many station weddings. One WAAF, not a packer, complained bitterly that men lost interest in her when they discovered that their lives did not depend on her skill! (Of all the fatal accidents which occurred during training, only one was due to an error in packing - proof of the dedication and expertise of the packers).

Parachute training was not the only interest of the Central Landing Establishment, as the unit came to be known. Other methods of transporting troops by air were also being developed, such as the use of gliders. (Gliders were of course eventually used in the D-Day landings.) However, experiments with gliders at Tatton Park began unpromisingly with a Hotspur glider sinking in Tatton Mere. Undeterred, the Glider School continued to operate until the end of 1940 when lack of space at Ringway forced it to move elsewhere. By then, parachute training was taking up all the available facilities. In 1942, the experimental section also left the airfield for the same reasons, but not before completing some interesting research on Rotachutes, Autogyros and glider development.

Despite the serious nature of its task, Ringway was a friendly place, as many people stationed there during those wartime years will testify.

Various changes took place here during the war. Concrete runways were constructed to combat poor weather conditions which often made the ground unserviceable. Buildings were covered with camouflage paint and even the grass was cut in camouflage patterns!

A number of important missions were carried out by members of the Airborne Forces. The first, code-named "Operation Colossus" was an experimental sabotage raid on the Tragino Aqueduct in Italy. The successful outcome of this operation proved the value of a small crack force parachuted into enemy territory to hit a specific target. Later, though, "Operation Market Garden" at Arnhem came to a tragic end with many lives lost. The most dramatic success came on D-Day when airborne troops were instrumental in establishing the Allies' bridgehead in France.

Leaving the Airport now, retrace the route to the A538. Turn left at the lights and after $1/2$ a mile left again to a pub called "THE ROMPER". Look for some older hangars close by which were once occupied by Fairey Aviation, a company already well established in the Manchester area, having had a factory at Heaton Chapel since 1934. It was here at Ringway that Fairey tested its "Battle" and "Barracuda" aircraft and later, the "Halifax" bombers.

You can imagine that in those strife-torn days, "The Romper" provided a welcoming and relaxed atmosphere for the parachute instructors and their pupils. It was here that they would get together after training to discuss informally the day's events. Although sticklers for Army etiquette might frown on instructors mixing with "other ranks" off-duty, the RAF instructors (whose branch of the Forces had a more relaxed attitude to off-duty activities) often got a more accurate picture of their pupils' reaction to the jump! And as a result, they were better able to judge trainees' suitability for the Airborne Forces.

From the pub, return to the A538 turn left; shortly after passing through the runway tunnel, turn left (signposted Quarry Bank Mill). On your left up the hill is the AVIATION VIEWING PARK where you can watch the aircraft at close range landing and taking off from the airport. There is an

Above: WAAFs at Ringway
Below: The "pillbox" near Styal.

aviation shop, refreshments and toilets. Open daily, all year.

Roughly 1½ miles further on, just past Oversley Cottages on the left, you can find a path beside a field leading to a kind of pillbox made of brick and concrete. This formed part of Ringway's defence and was used by an anti-aircraft crew stationed at nearby Morley.

Continue again towards STYAL and turn right at the junction with the main road, which can be found just beyond the Old Ship Inn. The Inn was used during wartime by the local Auxilliary Fire Service. QUARRY BANK MILL is situated a few hundred yards along on the right. Today, the mill is a major tourist attraction as a working textile mill and museum, but during the last war, it was somewhat run down and seems to have had little part to play in the war effort. However, evacuees were housed in the village and we know that some stayed at the APPRENTICE HOUSE, (now part of the museum) with the family who lived there. The Mill Manager was responsible for the Air Raid Wardens in the area, and the village's proximity to Ringway made this a task of vital importance.

You can visit Quarry Bank Mill daily (except Mondays in Winter). For more information, telephone Wilmslow 01625 527468.

Leaving Quarry Bank Mill, turn right and head towards Wilmslow. Then turn left on to the A34 Manchester Road and right at the Blue Bell traffic lights into Dean Row Road. Half a mile or so later, you will pass the site of RAF Wilmslow, a major training depot constructed during the war. Thousands of personnel underwent training here at various levels. Indeed, a WAAF who spent a week here on a course in RAF law, recalls the exhausting routine of early rising, an hour's drill and PT before breakfast, more drill between lectures and no time for relaxation before she fell into bed at night, utterly worn out!

Today the site of RAF Wilmslow (mainly on the right of Dean Row Road) has disappeared under new housing development. However, if you look carefully at the roads opposite, which are named after famous aircraft such as "Tudor", "Lancaster", "Lincoln" and "Anson", you will see the typically solid official style of the houses, evidence of the RAF's presence here.

At the end of Dean Row Road, we take the A5102 to WOODFORD. Travelling roughly 1$^1$/$_2$ miles further on, you can see on the right the former factory of A.V. Roe (now British Aerospace), once the home of that most famous and arguably best-loved aircraft of the war, the "Lancaster" bomber. Hundreds of Lancasters were made here

*WAAFs on a training course at Wilmslow.*

and flown from Woodford Aerodrome to bomber bases in the south-east of England.

Pilots of the Air Transport Auxilliary (ATA) would ferry newly completed aircraft to bomber squadrons. Ferry Pool Pilots in the ATA were often women, or men whose age excluded them from active duties. Tongue-in-cheek, they nicknamed themselves "Ancient and Tattered Airmen"!

Lancasters were often modified for special purposes. They were popular with their pilots for they were reliable and handled well. Their specification was consistent in all but a very few, a tribute to the efficiency of the production system.

Because of its range and reliability, the Lancaster was chosen for the famous Dambusters' raid on the Mohne Dam; a large hole was cut from the bottom of the fuselage to house the huge "Bouncing" bomb designed by Barnes Wallis. There were fears at the time that this would alter the wind resistance of the aircraft and affect its stability in the air but tests proved these reservations groundless. Once again the Lancaster's superb design was proved unbeatable.

British Aerospace at Woodford is not open to the public but there is an annual air show there, usually in late June.

Let's return towards Wilmslow from Woodford now and head for the main town shopping centre on the A34 Alderley Road. Behind Sainsbury's, in a small memorial garden stands the gypsy caravan which once belonged to "Romany", The Rev. Bramwell Evans, a popular wartime writer and broadcaster on countryside matters, who was extremely popular with his listeners, especially children.

Following the main road into Alderley Edge, a charming village which became "home" to many evacuees, turn left on to the B5087 Macclesfield Road. This leads uphill past the "Edge", a popular beauty spot. Turn left again and follow signs for Mottram St Andrew, which lies on the A538 some two miles east of Alderley Edge. During the war, MOTTRAM HALL (now a luxury country house hotel) housed many US Officers. Indeed, they and their men became familiar sights in the district as they enjoyed sight-seeing in this attractive part of Cheshire.

---

**OTHER PLACES TO VISIT:**

▶ *Adlington Hall Historic House, Adlington Tel: 01625 829206*

▶ *Brookside Miniature Railway and Garden Centre, Poynton Tel: 01625 872919*

---

*Lancaster bomber. (British Aerospace, Woodford).*

*The Lancaster production line at Woodford. (British Aerospace, Woodford).*

84

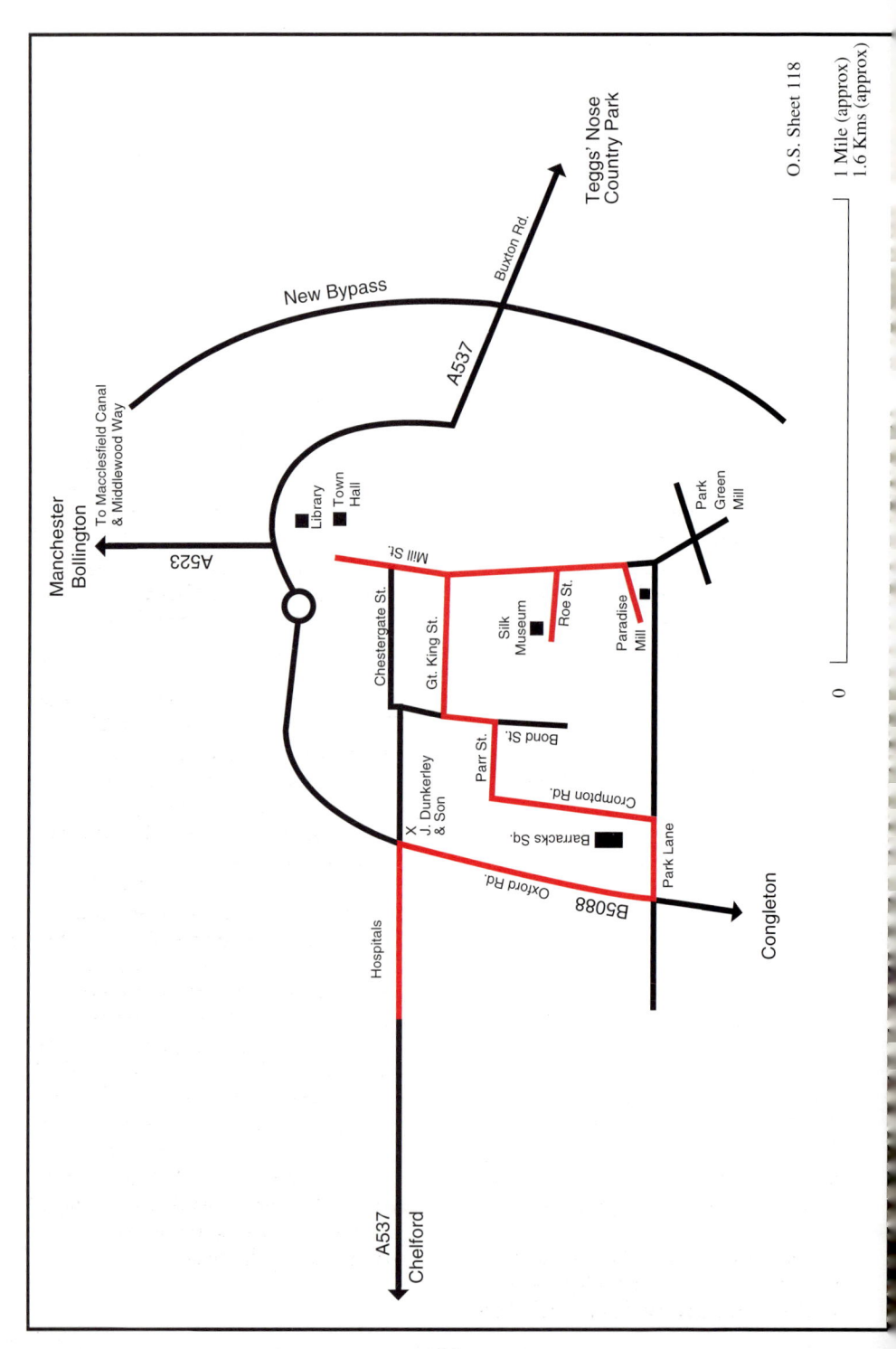

# Macclesfield at War

## Silk Mills and Stone Quarries

Macclesfield lies on the edge of the Pennines and is best known for the manufacture of silk. Today, though many of its mills lie silent and some house other industries, you can still imagine the steep cobbled streets of the town alive with the busy clatter of millworkers' clogs on their journey to and from work. During wartime these mills and their workers were to make a huge contribution to Britain's war effort, supplying yarn and finished cloth for the armed forces for uniforms, mosquito nets and, of course, silk for parachutes.

At the outbreak of World War II, Macclesfield was designated the centre of silk production, and the Silk and Rayon Control Board was established in The Dams and later, in the Brocklehurst Memorial Halls in Queen Victoria Street. In the early months, silk continued to be made for dress and furnishing fabrics, but later, supplies of raw silk were difficult to import and despite attempts to secure new sources of supply in India and Lebanon, the Government was forced to stipulate that the precious commodity could only be used for making parachutes, linings for airmen's gloves and surgical sutures.

Unlike workers in other key industries, the silk workers were not often required to work a seven day week, although there were some emergencies - such as the aftermath of Dunkirk when the forces urgently needed replacement supplies - when production had to be stepped up. Many of them now recall how hot the mills became in the blackout - though some factories did have blackout screens that could be rolled back during the day to allow light and air in.

Every firm was involved with the war effort. One, Olivers, produced $85^1/_2$ million miles of yarn for parachutes, mosquito nets and items of uniform. Challinor & Holmes - normally manufacturers of ribbon and trimmings - worked flat out to produce periphery tape for parachute edgings (capable of bearing a weight of 500 lbs). This tape was a "natural" colour and very different from the rainbow hues of the pre-war period that the women workers had been used to making. In spite of the dullness of their task, they responded magnificently to the responsibility placed upon them, and, like all those involved in parachute production and packing, were well aware that men's lives depended on the quality of their work. W. Frost & Son (Park Green and Union Mills) and Heath & Co also turned their factories over to parachute manufacture at this time.

Another firm, J Dunkerley & Son in Oxford Road, used its skill and technical expertise to develop insulating undersuits for divers and frogmen. These were used by the men who reconnoitred the French beaches in preparation for D-Day. The company also co-operated with Dunlop to produce the famous Franks Flying Suit (or Anti-G suit as it was sometimes called) which prevented airmen from suffering fatal blackouts at high altitudes.

According to the demands of Essential Work Orders, other companies adapted their production to suit wartime needs. Neckwear Limited, for example, produced white sweaters for sub-mariners at their Grosvenor Street Mill, while the Castle Shoe Company had to turn out a quota of ladies' shoes, to ensure supplies were adequate even after coupons were introduced. V & E Plastics' Victor Works in Derby Street produced electrical cable and equipment such as generator parts.

Many new employers came to the town at this time. Macclesfield was considered an unlikely target for German bombers and so industry could carry on safely there. The firm of Osband Bros moved from blitz-ravaged London and produced forces' clothing, like battledress and ARP uniforms. The former Macclesfield firm of Hovis returned for a time after the bombing of its new mill in Trafford Park, Manchester.

Thin strips of aluminium foil (called "Window" or "Angel's Hair" by the children of Occupied Europe) were produced at Vernons - owned by Mr Vernon Sangster. These were dropped from bombers to fool enemy Radar operators into believing that a large airborne force was approaching - a vital secret weapon, used in the Normandy invasion.

On the subject of secrets, another invention developed with the co-operation of Macclesfield's silk industry was a map printed on silk and issued to airmen and secret agents to help them escape from enemy territory to safety. Clayton Hutton, the inventor, had experimented with paper but this rustled, and creased so that the features became illegible. Then he thought of silk which was easily concealed inside clothing, but he had difficulty in obtaining silk samples to test this theory until he approached Mr Wallace Ellison, Manager of Brocklehurst Whiston Amalgamated at Langley, a village near Macclesfield, who supplied the first batch of trial squares. Mr Ellison was most sympathetic to the idea, for he himself had escaped from a prisoner of war camp in the Great War. The technique proved difficult to perfect as the printing inks "bled", until Hutton tried pectin to fix the colours, and this worked. Soon the maps were produced on a large scale for use in France and Germany, and the Far East. They were even printed on both sides after the silk had been impregnated with chalk.

*Silk handkerchief. (Macclesfield Silk Museum).*

Nowadays, it is impossible to trace every factory that contributed to the war effort, but on a visit to Macclesfield it is possible to see some of them and enjoy a pleasant stroll around the town.

As you approach Macclesfield on the A537 from Chelford on the Chester Road, look out for Parkside Hospital on the left and a little further on also on the left find West Park Hospital where many wounded men were treated throughout the war.

Let's turn right into Oxford Road at the next roundabout (B5088 to Congleton). Almost immediately on the left you will see the mill owned by J DUNKERLEY & SON. Here, as previously mentioned, they produced silk undersuits and flying suits, and yellow silk triangles for signalling which helped Allied troops to identify one another.

Continue on now along Oxford Road and turn left at the traffic lights into Park Lane, then second left into Crompton Road. See almost immediately on the left BARRACKS SQUARE - now turned into flats - originally 19th century barracks for the local militia. During the last war these were used by American troops, and tanks were a familiar sight on the parade ground.

Travel along Crompton Road for a quarter of a mile and turn right into Parr Street which leads into Athey Street. Here turn left into Bond Street and right into Great King Street where you can find parking, or follow signs for car parks in the town centre.

Let's take a walk through the centre of Macclesfield now, from the TOWN HALL where you can see the local roll of honour on display, down Mill Street, the main shopping area. If you have time, why not wander off to the left and find the steep twisting cobbled streets and steps which give the town its unique flavour.

Turn right off Mill Street into Roe Street where you will find the MACCLESFIELD SILK MUSEUM. Originally built as a non-denominational Sunday school by the founder, John Whitaker, it has been restored and modified to serve the local community and visitors to the area as a social and cultural centre. The Silk

*The Sunday School, now Macclesfield Silk Museum.*

Museum has exhibits on Macclesfield's major industry. There are also wartime items on show, including the escape maps mentioned previously and other items produced locally at the time. Open daily all year, you can telephone 01625 613210 for more information.

From here, let's go down Mill Street and at the foot of the hill, turn right into Park Lane. Before visiting Paradise Mill at the end of the lane, look straight ahead at Park Green. The mill building which faces you was one of those owned by Frosts, who produced parachutes.

PARADISE MILL (part of the Macclesfield Silk Museum) in Park Lane, demonstrates the art of Jaquard handloom silk weaving. You can see the mill as it was in the late 1930s and early 1940s

*Paradise Mill, Macclesfield. (Macclesfield Silk Heritage).*

with the original looms still in use. When it was owned by Cartwright and Sheldon, in the war years the workers wove parachute cloth and also began to use synthetic fibres such as nylon. Nylon was used for parachute cloth as silk supplies ran short - though its bulk was a disadvantage. The mill is open afternoons Tuesday to Sunday and Bank Holidays. For more details, telephone Macclesfield 01625 613210.

Our next place to visit is TEGG'S NOSE COUNTRY PARK so let's leave Macclesfield now and drive for about a mile on the Buxton Road (A537). Directional signs lead you to the Country Park of Teggs' Nose Quarry. During the war crushed stone was produced here to build concrete air raid shelters, and later to construct roadways in American camps in the county, like Marbury, Northwich, Peover, Knutsford and Winsford. Other local quarries at Kerridge and Stoneyfold produced stone for the aerodrome at Woodford. Stoneyfold also supplied silica stone for a Midlands steel works involved in making steel for Spitfire crankshafts.

Teggs' Nose itself has commanding views over the surrounding countryside. It was a Home Guard Post in the war and men on duty here could see Liverpool and Manchester ablaze after massive air raids. Although the Macclesfield area was not a primary target, the Home Guard and ARP wardens took their duties very seriously and the possibility of an attack seemed quite real. The Home Guard trained in earnest, although amusing incidents did occur to lighten the serious mood. Once, the local Home Guard impressed an inspection party of "Top Brass" from Chester with the accuracy of its fire on a demonstration exercise near here. A Smith gun, which could be turned on its side and rotated to aim at the target, was being tested on a First World War tank. The target in fact was blown up with precision timing by a guardsman with experience of quarrying explosives, who lay out of sight in a trench. The resultant

Smith gun.

"Hit" was very impressive, especially as it was enhanced with additional dust from a bag of white powder placed alongside the charge!

There were a number of false alarms. In retrospect, these must have seemed quite amusing! One story tells of the night a terrified sentry reported to his comrades that he had seen a parachutist. Since an airborne landing by the enemy was Britain's greatest fear - and the main reason why guards were posted in remote places such as this - the group went to investigate. The situation was even more tense for they had only six rounds of ammunition between them. Nervously they approached the white mass which could be seen behind a wall, and crawled cautiously towards it. As they peered over the wall, fear turned to relief and some embarrassment when they discovered that the "parachute" was no more than a load of lime dumped there by a farmer!

The park at Tegg's Nose is a great place for a walk but take sensible shoes with you for the ground is rather rough. If you walk from the car park to the old quarry, the path leads you past Crooked Yard Farm. In the field to the left of the farmhouse, you can see a hollow in the ground - a souvenir of a stray flying bomb which fell here on Christmas Eve 1944 during the only flying bomb raid on the North West.

There is a display of old quarrying equipment here, some wartime examples

Quarry machinery, Tegg's Nose Country Park.

*Troop train near Rose Hill.*

among them. These were used in a time when Teggs' Nose stone was in great demand for military purposes, and trucks were a familiar sight as they groaned their way all day along the uneven dusty tracks carrying away their loads of crushed stone Teggs' Nose Country Park is open daily. You can obtain refreshments at the visitors' centre at weekends and Bank holidays WEATHER PERMITTING and the rangers will be pleased to tell you more about the area. Contact Macclesfield (01625) 614279 for more details.

The MIDDLEWOOD WAY and the MACCLESFIELD CANAL are also conveniently located for visitors to Macclesfield. Both can be joined at the village of Bollington, at Grimshaw Lane just off the B5090, east of the A523.

The Middlewood Way, an 11 mile country trail stretching from Macclesfield to Marple, has been created from a disused railway line. Nowadays a peaceful public footpath and cycleway with several access points, you will find a picnic area at the former Higher Poynton station. Many interesting plants and flowers grow here and as it is level, it is ideal for those who prefer less strenuous walking.

The Macclesfield, Bollington and Marple Railway (as it was in wartime) was used for freight and passenger transport but also carried troops and supplies. Here as elsewhere the war put additional pressure on railway staff - especially when men were called up. Women were often brought in to replace the men in essential jobs such as portering. On the Macclesfield - Marple line, Mrs Gladys Parker became the signalwomen at Middlewood High Level signal box, now demolished. Middlewood Station has vanished now although the Way is named after it. Some interesting features of railway history can be seen on the Way as well as sights like White Nancy (a folly on the hill above Bollington) and Bollington

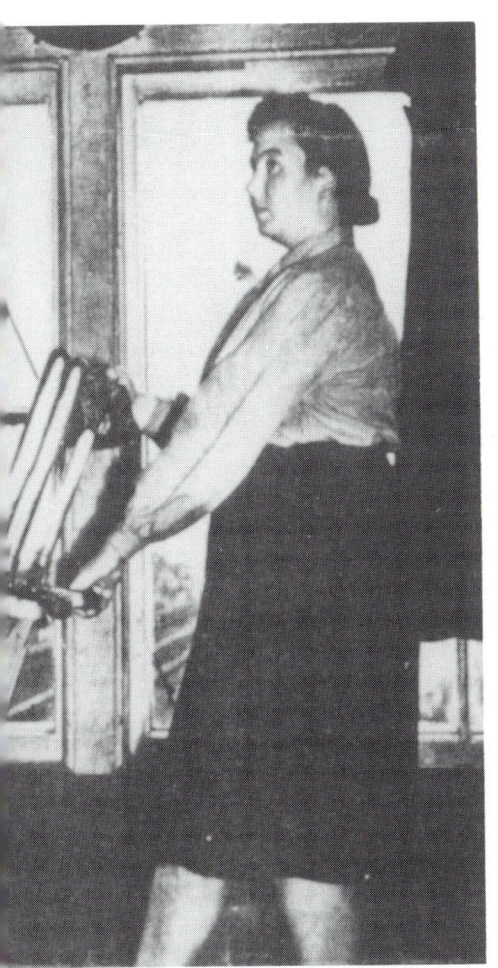

*Mrs G. Parker - Middlewood High Level Signalwomen.*

Aqueduct. You will find information boards at the main access points where the Way is crossed by road bridges and rangers will be pleased to answer your questions on the area. For more information, telephone Bollington 01625 573998 or Macclesfield Borough Council Leisure Services on 01625 500500

The towpath of the Macclesfield Canal forms part of the CHESHIRE RING CANAL WALK, (Guide booklets are available from some Cheshire libraries and information centres) which covers almost 100 miles. Like the Middlewood Way, running almost parallel with it, the Walk is accessible at several points, including Bollington and Buxton Road, Macclesfield - not far from Teggs' Nose.

Wartime precautions were taken seriously on the canal network. Stop-planks (you can see them stored along the banks) and stop-gates could be used to block the canal at certain points along its length to prevent a disastrous loss of water if the bank was breached for any reason, such as enemy bombing. At various points along the towpath, usually by bridges, look for reinforced grooves cut into the bank where planks could be dropped into position in such an emergency. During the war lock-keepers and other canal workers carried out this duty and had to be available at all times in case of a raid. Anxiety about possible airborne invasion was always present and brought special precautions. Pillboxes were built to protect strategic points and some of these survive today. You can still see one at Bridge 13 on the Macclesfield Canal and another at Bosley Reservoir, between Macclesfield and Congleton.

*OTHER PLACES TO VISIT:*

▶ *Bollington Discovery Centre - environmental exhibition; cycle hire. Tel: 01625 572681*

▶ *Dunge Farm Gardens, Kettleshulme. Tel: 01663 733787*

▶ *Gawsworth Hall, near Macclesfield Tel: 01260 223456*

▶ *Flora Flower Gift and Garden Centre, near Macclesfield. Tel: 01625 422418*

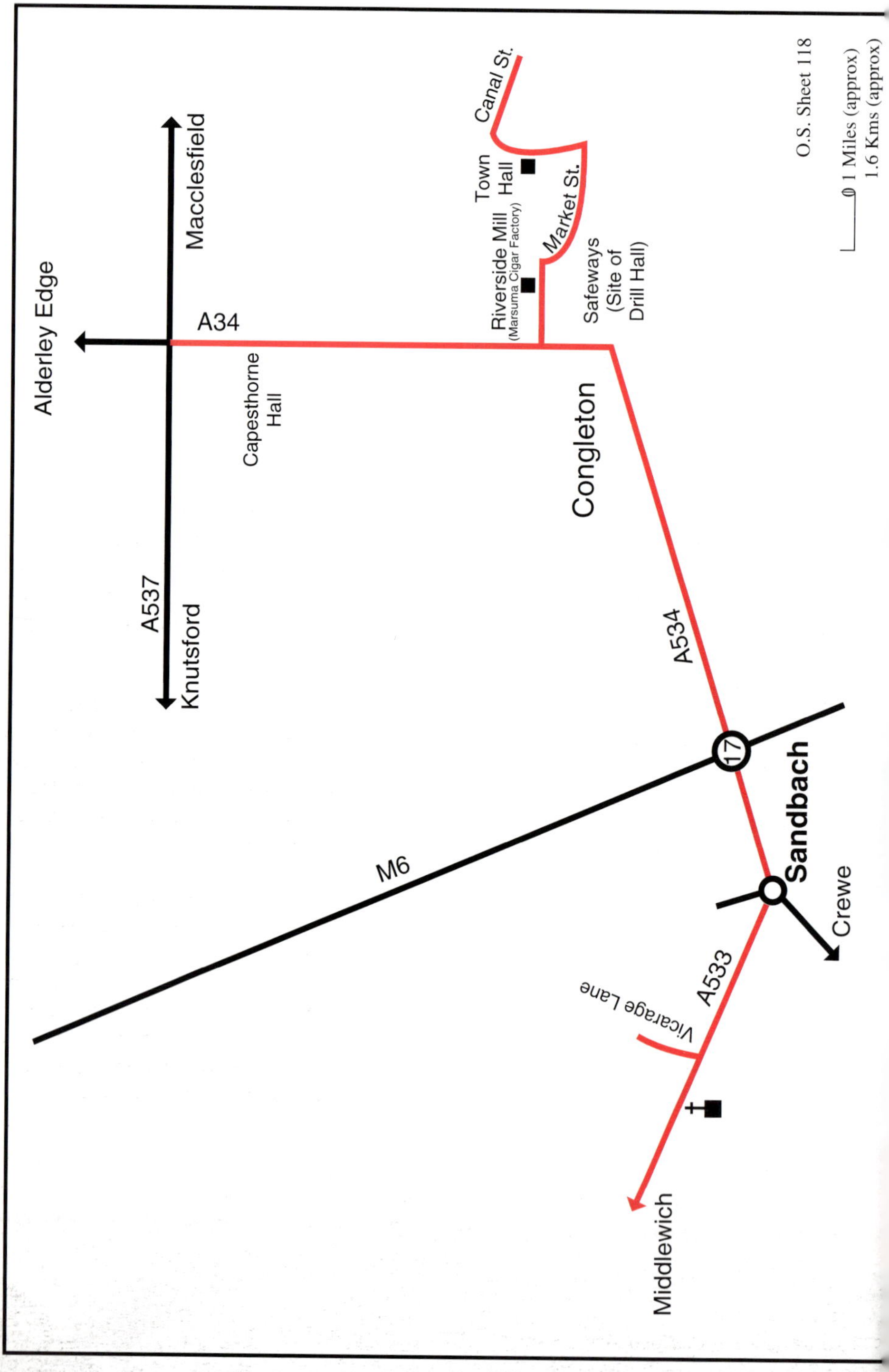

Alderley Edge
Macclesfield
A34
A537
Knutsford
Capesthorne Hall
Riverside Mill (Marsuma Cigar Factory)
Town Hall
Canal St.
Market St.
Safeways (Site of Drill Hall)
Congleton
A534
17
Sandbach
M6
Crewe
A533
Vicarage Lane
Middlewich
O.S. Sheet 118
0 1 Miles (approx)
1.6 Kms (approx)

# Capesthorne, Congleton and Sandbach

## *Convalescents, Dutchmen and Vehicles of War*

Between Macclesfield and Crewe lie the market towns of Congleton and Sandbach. Both made very different contributions to the war effort. Congleton was to play host to Dutch troops who escaped from Holland and the Nazi Occupation, while Sandbach would produce many military vehicles - tanks included - which would see service in every theatre of war.

Our tour takes us first a few miles north of Congleton to CAPESTHORNE HALL, a lovely 18th and 19th century mansion. Capesthorne was also to play a valuable role in the war, enabling wounded men to recuperate in the peace of the Cheshire countryside.

You will find Capesthorne Hall on the A34, one mile south of the A537. It has been the home of the Bromley-Davenport family for generations. During the war, it was made available to the Red Cross and St John's Ambulance Brigade for use as a convalescent home. Facilities here catered for about sixty men at a time, although numbers varied.

It was here that the wounded would come for a few weeks' recovery from a military hospital in Chester where they had received initial treatment. Before they left, they would have to be fit enough to walk for two miles carrying a full kit.

To make way for beds, the furniture was cleared out of the main reception rooms, the Saloon and Drawing Room, and the Dining Room became a recreation room for the men. For entertainment, they could play billiards or listen to the radio or gramophone. Capesthorne had its own theatre and local amateurs often

*Capesthorne Hall.*

performed pantomimes there. There were also visits from ENSA. All this must have done wonders to relieve the boredom of convalescence, for there were few visitors owing to the difficulties of travel in wartime and the distance the men were from their homes.

Sir William Bromley-Davenport even gave the men permission to fish in the lake close to the house - with interesting results! A large pike was caught one day and presented to the Red Cross cook, who agreed to prepare it for dinner. The pike was duly placed in the cold larder until it was time to bake it. Suddenly a thumping sound disturbed the kitchen staff, who were horrified to find that the fish had merely been stunned and was flopping around on the floor of the larder!

Although it was out of bounds to leave the Park (even to visit the local pub), patients could wander at will around the grounds. (Their convalescents' uniform of blue suit and red tie would have made them rather conspicuous anyway!)

*A favourite fishing spot, the lake at Capesthorne.*

General Patton (who resided at Peover Hall, not far away) was kind enough to arrange a baseball game on the lawn at the rear of the house for the patients' entertainment. The beds were wheeled out into the garden for the men to watch and everyone seems to have had a marvellous day!

*Patients enjoy the fresh air at Capesthorne.*

Other distinguished visitors to Capesthorne at that time included the Princess Royal (Princess Mary), Edwina, Lady Mountbatten and Lady Stamford.

The staff lived in various bedrooms and had their own private sitting room. On the first floor, you can see the Dorothy Davenport Room, (once used by the Matron), the Blue Dressing Room (formerly the office) and the small State Bedroom (used as a consulting room for the visiting doctor).

Capesthorne was a happy place, thanks to the kindness and efficiency of successive Commandants, notably Mrs Baskerville-Glegg, Mrs Walter Bromley-Davenport and Mrs Clark. It continued also as a family home for Sir William Bromley-Davenport and his sister, as well as housing some evacuees at the Kennels, next door to the Hall.

*Mrs Walter Bromley-Davenport with patients at Capesthorne.*

*American visitors at Capesthorne, ready to watch some baseball.*

The only occurrence to temporarily mar the peace of Capesthorne at this time was a landmine which exploded in the park, but fortunately there were no casualties. The residents of Capesthorne - in common with the rest of their countrymen - were well prepared for the worst. Blackout regulations were strictly observed and there were sandbags around the courtyard. Regular fire drills took place which included clambering over the roof to check for incendiary bombs.

Apart from the fascinating rooms in the Hall, the gardens and the park, Capesthorne also has a lovely chapel. (This was used in wartime by the family, the patients and the staff.) Telephone 01625 861779 for opening times.

Taking leave of Capesthorne now, continue on the A34 into Congleton and turn left at the traffic lights on the hill for the town centre. Continue over the bridge to the roundabout and on your left you will see RIVERSIDE MILL formerly the Marsuma Cigar Factory where Dutch troops were billeted on their arrival in the town in the late summer of 1940. It, along with other premises in Canal Street (Albion Mill) and the Drill Hall had been in use since the outbreak of war for territorial troops and conscripts, who were being trained in the area. Later they were to house the Americans.

Turn right, opposite Riverside Mill where there is convenient parking if you wish to explore the town centre. On the site of Safeway was the old Drill Hall and if you climb up the slope into the shopping centre, you can turn left to see the TOWN HALL, the scene of much work for the local war effort. Turn right opposite it into Canal Street, and you will find the former ALBION MILL, now offices.

Street "Victory" party in Congleton. (Congleton Chronicle).

St Nicholas visiting Dutch troops - Congleton, December 1940. (Imperial War Museum).

96

*"Salute the Soldier" Week in Congleton. (Congleton Chronicle).*

*Sgt. Eardley with General Montgomery. (Courtesy of Congleton Chronicle).*

The Dutch troops mentioned previously were destined to spend nine months in Congleton. In January 1941 they were formed into Princess Irene's Brigade, later to move to Wolverhampton. Later still, they were to land at Nijmegen to help in the liberation of Holland.

The Dutch soldiers were very popular and many later married Congleton girls. Today the link still survives for Congleton is "twinned" with Oosterhout in the Netherlands and there is a Dutch Association in the town.

Congleton, like so many other towns, did not escape the effects of the war, but it was lucky not to suffer any serious air raids. Perhaps this was just as well as the town's water supply was known to be less than adequate. It seems the organisers of the emergency services were constantly trying to have the water pressure improved but did not succeed in this until after the war had ended.

People in Congleton - like those all over the county - made the best of things. They contributed generously to "Warship Weeks" and "Salute the Soldier" funds. They were especially proud of the town's

Victoria Cross holder - Sgt Harold Eardley - and gave him a tumultous hero's welcome on his return home. Eardley, who died in 1991, won his medal in the Netherlands in 1944 when, having lost seven of his men to German machine gun fire, he destroyed three gun posts which had been holding up the advance of the Allies towards the German border. Today, there is a street named after this courageous man who was also awarded eleven other medals, and the Croix de Guerre from the French.

*Prince Bernhard visited Dutch troops in Congleton.*

Despite the lack of labour due to conscription, work in Congleton continued. Firms such as Berisfords (who produced ribbons and tape for medals and uniforms) carried on as best they could. Local workers, many of them women, produced components for firms such as Fodens at Sandbach. Others aided the war effort more directly making ammunition at an ordnance factory near Alsager.

Let's leave Congleton now by taking the A534 for SANDBACH which is approximately 6 miles drive to the west.

Perhaps the town's main attraction until recently has been the Saxon stone crosses which stand in an old cobbled square in the town centre. Sandbach is not only the home of an excellent weekly market, but it is also the birthplace of the internationally known Foden and ERF vehicles. (Interestingly, although they are separate companies, they were set up by different branches of the same family).

Seven and a half million shells were produced, mainly by women, at the Foden

# Glossary

**AACU**  Anti-Aircraft Calibration Unit.

**Ack Ack**  Anti-Aircraft (guns).

**All Clear**  Siren rate used at the end of an air raid to indicate danger was past.

**ARP**  Air Raid Precautions.

**ATA**  Air Transport Auxilliary.

**ATS**  Auxilliary Territorial Service (now WRAC).

**Axis powers**  Originally Germany and Italy, later joined by Japan.

**BEF**  British Expeditionary Force.

**DZ**  Dropping Zone.

**ENSA**  Entertainments National Services Association.

**FANY**  First Aid Nursing Yeomanry.

**Home Guard**  Originally the LDV, the 'Home Guard' or 'Dad's Army' were recruited from older men and young men who were unable to serve in the Forces. Their task was to protect and defend the country against invasion, although they were often poorly equipped.

**ICI**  Imperial Chemical Industries (originally Brunner Mond).

**LDV**  Local Defence Volunteers (later Home Guard).

**Lend Lease**  The arrangement between Britain and the USA, early in the war whereby the US supplied ships and equipment on favourable financial terms.

**LMS**  London, Midland and Scottish (Railway).

**MAP**  Ministry of Aircraft Production.

**Munich Crisis**  The meeting in 1938 when the British P.M. Neville Chamberlain agreed to allow Hitler to take over part of Czechoslovakia. This averted war for a time and enabled Britain to prepare for it.

**NAAFI**  Navy, Army and Air Force Institute - organisation providing service people's canteens; a canteen itself.

**Pillbox**  Small, concrete reinforced hut used to protect troops.

**PLUTO**  PipeLine Under The Ocean.

**PTS**  Parachute Training School.

**RADAR**  Radio Detection And Ranging equipment, used to detect the enemy or to establish one's own position by measuring radio pulses.

**SLG**  Satellite Landing Ground.

**SOE**  Special Operations Executive (a section which trained secret agents and sent them into enemy territory).

**USAAF**  United States Army Air Force.

**WAAF**  Women's Auxilliary Air Force - a member was known as a 'Waaf'.

**War Ag**  War Agricultural Executive Committee - each local committee could order families to grow certain crops or keep certain numbers of livestock, and had power to dispossess any who did not co-operate.

**WD**  War Department.

**Western Command**  One of the military divisions of the country. H.Q. was at Chester.

**WLA**  Women's Land Army.

**WVS**  Women's Voluntary Service (now WRVS).

**YMCA**  Young Men's Christian Association.

*Women making shells at Fodens. (E. Foden Transport Museum).*

works at Elworth. Here they also produced Centaur and Crusader tanks for the armed forces, and nearly 2000 WD vehicles, heavy duty lorries and trucks which had to withstand the punishing conditions of desert warfare. The works had its own Home Guard, Decontamination Squad and Fire Service. Some members of Foden's Fire Service even went to help fight the flames of the Manchester blitz. Fodens did not forget

*Foden W.D. lorries on Middlewich Road, Sandbach. (Fodens)*

their employees serving in the forces - an allowance was paid to them and parcels of comforts were sent out regularly.

To round off this tour, you can continue along the A533 towards MIDDLEWICH. Here the road runs alongside the Trent and Mersey Canal, popular with people taking narrow boat cruises for pleasure. Look out for the gaily painted boats which are often to be seen on this stretch of waterway, which leads to Middlewich, and beyond to the Anderton Lift at Northwich.

### OTHER PLACES TO VISIT
- ▶ *The Potters Barn, Hassall Green, Tel: 01270 884080*
- ▶ *Dukes Oak Gallery (Arts Centre), Brereton Tel: 01477 532337*